MISSION
OF THE
UNIVERSITY

Foundations of Higher Education
David S. Webster, Series Editor

MISSION
OF THE
UNIVERSITY

José Ortega y Gasset

Edited and Translated by
Howard Lee Nostrand

With a New Introduction by
Clark Kerr

Transaction Publishers
New Brunswick (U.S.A.) and London (U.K.)

Third printing 2001

New material this edition copyright © 1992 by Transaction Publishers, New Brunswick, New Jersey 08903. Originally published in 1944 by Princeton University Press.

This book is printed on acid-free paper that meets the American National Standard for Permanence of Paper for Printed Library Materials.

Library of Congress Catalog Number: 91-11561
ISBN: 1-56000-560-2
Printed in the United States of America

Library of Congress Cataloging-in-Publication Data

Ortega y Gasset, José, 1883–1955.
   [Misión de la universidad. English]
   Mission of the university / José Ortega y Gasset; edited and translated by Howard Lee Nostrand; with a new introduction by Clark Kerr.
   p.   cm.
   Translation of Misón de la universidad.
   Includes bibliographical references and index.
   ISBN 1-56000-560-2
   1. Education, Higher—Aims and objectives. 2. Universities and colleges—History. 3. Educational change. I. Nostrand, Howard Lee, 1910– . II. Title.
LB2321.07513   1991
378'.01—dc20   91-11561
                                              CIP

CONTENTS

TO THE F. U. E. OF MADRID

The Federación Universitaria Escolar of Madrid asked me to give a lecture on some topic related to the reform of higher education. The very poor acoustics of the Paraninfo, however, and my poor health at the time, prevented me from developing adequately the theme of my lecture. This circumstance prompted me afterward to rewrite somewhat more amply the notes I had taken with me to the Paraninfo. And here you have the result. It will be seen that except for an introduction, which the student mind of that time made necessary, I have kept rigorously to what I consider the crucial question. I was anxious to advance this question for discussion, and the pages which follow make no pretense of being anything more than the material for an extensive debate. Accordingly, I have set down my ideas with exaggerated sharpness and simplicity.

In no respect do I flatter myself that I have treated the theme of higher education with any sort of adequacy. The present essay is to be considered only as an anticipation of some future course on the Idea of the University. A definitive study calls first of all for a clear description of the essential characteristics of our age and an accurate diagnosis of the rising generation.

Introduction to the
Transaction Edition

THERE is no such thing as *the* one and only mission of *the* one and only university. There never has been, is not now, and never will be. There are, instead, several, even many, competing missions, and several, even many, types of institutions of higher education. Ortega himself set forth four missions for the Spanish-type university.

Having said that, let me quickly add that Ortega has *a* mission (one among his four) that warrants serious consideration by many universities and other institutions of higher education, and that this mission should be of more interest in the United States in the future than it has been over the more than half a century since Ortega first advanced it. This mission is an answer to the question: what is the knowledge most worth knowing by all students? Or, to put it in more common terms: what should be the content of a "liberal education"? The answer he gives is not the "Great Books," not "Western Civilization," not "World Civilization," not "distribution requirements," and not "race, gender, and class" all by itself. It is, in my judgment, a better answer than any of these, and I shall set it forth below as I understand it and shall try to apply it to the twenty-first century.

The Historical Context

Ortega set forth his "mission of the university" in a series of lectures at the University of Madrid in 1930. Time and place and Ortega himself are important to an understanding of his vision.

The time was the end of the dictatorship of General Primo de Rivera in Spain and the prospect for a democracy that turned out, so sadly, to be of shorter life than then hoped for and expected by its supporters, including Ortega, who served as a member of the new Constituent Assembly.

Ortega's six addresses were given at the invitation and under the auspices of the Student Federation. He was telling the students what he thought they should have available to study in the curriculum in order to live their own lives to the fullest and to contribute their best to the leadership of the nation.

Ortega viewed the Spanish university at that time as a "sad, inert, dispirited thing" but emphasized that the "moment is full of opportunity."[1] Spain and its citizens and its institutions, he then thought, were positioned at the "dawn of an illustrious era"; the "horizon which lies open . . . is a magnificent one"; and there was a "magnificent opportunity for thorough reforms of the Spanish state and university."

It was one of those times in history, as expressed by Alexander Pope in his *Essay on Man*, written in the period after the "Glorious Revolution" in England, when it could be said with some conviction that "hope springs eternal in the human breast." In Spain, however, six years after 1930, Generalissimo Francisco Franco came marching out of North Africa and the University of Madrid became a center of prolonged and bloody fighting. Some of the students of 1930 were casualties. But 1930 was a time for dreams and Ortega shared his with the students at Madrid.

The dream of democracy did come true again after the death of Franco, although Ortega stood uncommitted and uninvolved during the Spanish Civil War. I do not really understand why, except, perhaps, that he may have seen it as a contest between fascism and communism and he detested both.[2] The dream of a better university, however, has not come true at all and the Spanish university could be described today in terms reminiscent of those used in 1930 by Ortega.

Ortega

Ortega (1883-1955) studied in Jesuit schools and at the University of Madrid, and then at Leipzig, Berlin, and Marburg. From 1910 to 1936 he was a professor of moral philosophy at the University of Madrid.

He was a political liberal who opposed the Rivera dictatorship and supported the establishment of the Second Republic. He was, however, a very elitist liberal. Society, he thought, consisted of the masses and the classes (*The Revolt of the Masses*)[3], which meant to him those unqualified to lead (the masses) and those qualified to lead (the classes); and university students fell into the later category, which gave them very special responsibilities. And Spain then especially needed talented elites: "for the mass will not let itself be led, and what is left of the directing minority does not know how to lead."[4] Spain and the continent of Europe were on their way "back to barbarism."[5]

As a philosopher, Ortega sounds to me like a proto-existentialist: "life is what we do and what happens to us," and "I am myself plus my circumstance, and if I do not save it, I cannot save myself."[6]

Each of the above circumstances and orientations affected Ortega's approach to the university.

1. Madrid was a traditional Spanish university. That meant it followed Salamanca as Salamanca had earlier followed Bologna in becoming mostly a series of professional schools–law, medicine, and engineering in particular–with some Aristotle

added. When Ortega wrote about the "mission of the university," he accepted the training of professionals as one mission. So his first mission was the historical Madrid mission: "The Teaching of the Learned Professions."

2. The German universities where Ortega studied followed the Humboldt model of emphasis on research. The Spanish universities did not. Ortega thought they should. He thus also endorsed the German mission: "Scientific Research and the Preparation of Future Investigators."

3. As a political liberal, Ortega favored a democracy, but a democracy needed leaders. These leaders were most likely to come from the professional levels of society, which he called the "directive class of society." Members of this "directive class" thus required more than an education in the skills of their professions; they also required an education so that they might "govern." The members of the learned professions, with their responsibilities to govern, needed to be educated for these responsibilities. Thus Ortega's third mission was training for political leadership. Ortega recognized that "workingmen" in a democracy also could be advantaged by some general education but he never suggested how this might be made available to them and implied that it would not be by the university, which was for the "learned professions."

4. I have called Ortega a proto-existentialist: each person has an opportunity, and even a duty, to direct his or her own life. "Every human being, perforce, picks his way through life." He quotes Leonardo da Vinci as saying, "who cannot what he will, let him will what he can." And the university should teach the student what he or she "needs to know to live his life"; should help create "a cultured person: to put him at the height of the times." To be there, each person must "have acquired some idea of the world and the things in it"; must "make an intellectual interpretation of the world"; must comprehend "the culture of

the age." Otherwise a person is condemned "to a lower life, more difficult, toilsome, unrefined"—"to the life of an infra-man." Thus, Ortega's fourth mission: to create "a cultured man [who] sees the paths of life in a clear light." In *Meditations on Quixote*,[7] he wrote that "man reaches his full capacity when he acquires complete consciousness of his circumstances."

"General Culture"

Ortega said he was not trying to create a universal model for the university based on the four assignments of training for the learned professions, research, preparation for leadership, and inculcation of an understanding of surrounding circumstances. Nor did he want to follow any other country's model: "imitation would be fatal." In particular, he did not accept the English model, which "preserved the nonprofessional aspect of the university," nor the German with its excessive emphasis on research: "let no one come and tell me that the German university . . . is a model." He wanted instead a special Spanish solution and said that universities "are only a part of a larger entity . . . [of] the whole nation which creates and maintains them." Nevertheless, his emphasis on "general culture" really knows no national boundaries or time limits; and it could fit, to one degree or another, into any national system of higher education and at any time. "General culture" was essential to both the third and fourth of his missions: preparation for leadership and for picking one's "way through life."

What did he mean by "general culture"? Let me quote him:

> the system of ideas, concerning the world and humanity, which the man of that time possesses

the essential system of ideas concerning the world and man which belong to our times

the system of the vital ideas, which the age has attained

culture is the system of ideas . . . by which an age conducts its life

our active convictions as to the nature of our world and our fellow creatures

a system of live ideas which represents the superior level of the age

[comprehending] the gigantic world of today in which the life of the individual must be articulated

treating the great themes of the day.

This might all be identified, in the language of today, as the "Great Ideas" and/or the "Great Issues," and/or the "Great Themes" of our times. This is not the "Great Books." Ortega speaks contemptuously of "archaic ideas" and would, presumably, also so speak of "archaic issues."

His "general culture" is actually what the great Greek philosophers taught–Socrates, Plato, Aristotle. They also were concerned with the "great ideas" and "great issues" of their times when the city–state with "citizens" was being created for the first time in history: with justice, with the good society, with who should rule, with the responsibilities of citizenship, with how citizens should be reared and educated–all this, in the words of Aristotle, was "morally edifying." Aristotle was also concerned with research and almost single-handedly got biological science off to a good start. It was left to the Sophists to teach skills–including logic and rhetoric–which were, again quoting Aristotle, "practically useful."

The closest approximation to "general culture" in today's academic debates might appear to be an emphasis on "gender, race, and class," but I am sure Ortega would reject this as too narrow a definition of the "great ideas" and "great issues" of today. The Ortega approach, I would presume, would involve a more comprehensive listing, but he would be selective: "the knowledge which has to be acquired is out of proportion to the capacity to learn." He called this "the principle of economy in education."

The subject matter Ortega specifically lists as most important includes general knowledge of

> "the physical scheme of the world,"
> "organic life,"
> the "historical process"–"a decently coherent picture of the great movements of history,"
> "social life," and
> the "plan of the universe" (whatever that ay be?–but remember that Ortega had attended Jesuit schools).[8]

He did not include "science" in the sense of methods of investigation but only in the presentation of the *results* of investigation and their "impact for human life"–"the man of science . . . is . . . a barbarian knowing much of one thing."

Certain corollaries followed from this vision of "general culture" as seen by Ortega:

> that the curriculum would be student centered, not faculty centered;

that faculty members would need a "genius for integration," not the "pulverization of research," and "selection of professors will depend . . . on their talent for synthesis";

that the curriculum would be "inflexible in its requirements" (mostly required courses);

that a "faculty of culture" would be at the center of the university;

that "the university must assert itself as a major spiritual power" standing against "freezy," "frivolity," and "stupidity," must be an "uplifting force in the history of the western world" and a source for the "integration of knowledge, which today lies in pieces."

Ortega did raise the question of whether it would take "varied institutions,"–some differentiation of functions among institutions–rather than a single type of institution (the university), to comprehend his four missions, but only said that "scientific investigation proper is to be eliminated from the core of the university" and placed, instead, in "laboratories." The university proper would teach the "ordinary student to be a cultured person and a good member of a profession."

Great Ideas and Great Issues
for the Next Generation

How might one go about applying Ortega's vision to higher education in the twenty-first century? Such an effort might start by looking at the curriculum in Plato's Academy and in Aristotle's Lyceum–what great ideas and great issues did they select and why? Or at the attempt of Thomas Aquinas, who sought to combine Greek philosophy and the Bible? Perhaps, a search could also be made of the choices made when Napoleon reorganized the French system of higher education, or when the Humboldt model was selected in Germany, or at the time of the land-grant movement in the United States, or when the new universities were created after the Meiji Restoration in Japan, or in the U.S.S.R. after the Revolution of 1917–all of these were conscious attempts at a new examination of what should best be taught. But the twenty-first century will have different needs.

Another start might be made by listing the expected "great ideas" and "great issues" prospectively facing the next generation so that students might better be able to cope with the challenges of the new age–to understand these challenges and to analyze competitive responses to them.

Certainly "gender, race, and class" would be on the list but would not be the only items to be considered. Ortega, in 1930, certainly would have placed the consequences of the "Revolt of the Masses" on the agenda as a "great theme." Other illustrative alternative subjects that might be listed for consideration are

> the roles of religion and nationality in modern life;
> issues of war and peace, and the general subject of conflict resolution;
> the pathologies of industrial civilization;
> the implications of the "information revolution";
> the future of the environment–including the impacts of the population explosion;
> the prospects for Third World nations;
> new mentalities and new cultures that are now arising;
> the failure of Marxist-Leninist states and economies, and their problems of transition to new forms of society;
> competition in the global economy;
> comparative cultures of the world;
> decision-making processes.

Other related issues to be examined would be:

Should only one theme be chosen, or several? (I favor several.)

What should this theme or these themes be?

Should students be given a choice among themes? (I favor choice.)

How much of the curriculum should be allotted to this theme or themes? (I favor about one quarter to one third at the undergraduate level for "liberal education" in a four-year institution.)

Who should make the above decisions?

How can faculty members be persuaded to teach these broader themes, rather than solely their specialties?

How can research be applied to broad issues rather than only to narrow problems one at a time?

Should there be new mechanisms to administer the new approach? Ortega proposed, as noted above, a "faculty of culture."

Should there be an effort to reach the total population with "general culture"? (My answer is "absolutely yes," and this answer requires reliance on several institutions–including the high schools–and not the university alone.)

What should be the definition of the "age" to be studied? I have suggested an illustrative list of great issues for the next generation. This follows the lead of Ortega. He writes about "the historical world of his own generation"[9]–the period of each person's own life. He suggested, in particular, the importance of a fifteen-year period when each generation has "fifteen years of rule" between the ages of forty-five and sixty and of the fifteen years before that of "initiation."[10] By implication, the university should prepare the student for participation in the life of society between the ages of thirty to sixty years of age. But Ortega recognized that each period carries within itself both residues of the past and the seeds of the future.

To my knowledge, none of the more than twenty-four hundred nonspecialized institutions of higher education in the United States has considered such an effort of analysis and planning for a curriculum centered on "general culture."

My own evaluation of Ortega's proposal follows:

> It merits very careful consideration. Among other contributions it would give students a "broad learning experience."[11] to go along with specialization, helping them to think horizontally as well as vertically; and, well done, it would be very relevant to their lives.
>
> If Ortega's "mission" is chosen from among the several alternatives, then the selection of the theme or themes–and I strongly favor several themes with some choice by students among them, is of great importance. The choice made should be on academic and not on other grounds. I have doubts about "gender, race, and class,"

not as one theme among several, but as the one and only theme without careful consideration of alternatives. There seems to me to have been a recent rush to judgment uncharacteristic of academic life in some places.

Whatever themes are chosen, it should be realized that teaching outside the rigorous standards of departments has its dangers–that relevance may overwhelm rigor; and that the most careful choice of teaching materials will be necessary. Each theme should be treated with as much rigor as possible.

The emphasis should be on purpose: "treating the great themes of the day"; and the curriculum should thus be flexible in content as these great themes change in their configurations.

The analysis of each theme should be not only for its own sake but also to give students an experience in thinking critically and constructively about great issues of the age more generally–how to approach their study, how to formulate thoughtful responses.

The Missions of Higher Education

Finally I should like to place Ortega on a great map that includes many places. Each place on this map represents a view of what *should* mostly be done in higher education (what *is* done in actuality is another question).

Illustrative Dominant Single Central
Assignments for The University:

> Great themes of the current age: the great Greek philosophers.

Great ideas of past ages:[12] Robert Maynard Hutchins[13] ("The Great Books") and his many followers; also the Confucian "classics." This model asserts that the great ideas have already been discovered and written down, and that the main purpose of education is to pass on this traditional wisdom to future generations.

Training for leadership: John Henry Cardinal Newman,[14] writing in Britain and in the mid-nineteenth century, was the greatest advocate of "liberal education," one that prepares a man "to fill any post with credit."

New knowledge: The modern German research university, beginning with the founding of the University of Berlin in 1809, approached the discovery of truth and knowledge in all fields on the basis of scientific principles, joining the rational and empirical traditions to form the basis of modern scientific research. In the United States, the theme was taken up by Abraham Flexner and exemplified in his famous reforms of medical teaching.[15]

High professional training: The Sophists of ancient Greece, in contrast to Socrates and Plato and Aristotle, were principally concerned with supplying men to fill public posts through training in rhetoric. This professional model was also dominant in Italy and Spain, beginning in the late Middle Ages, as physicians, lawyers, priests, and accountants for church and state were educated in the universities of Bologna, Salamanca, and elsewhere. In the United States, Benjamin Franklin was the great advocate of the "most useful" knowledge.[16] In the late nineteenth and early twentieth centuries, the Imperial universities of Japan, founded after the Meiji Restoration, concentrated on training an elite corps of students for the nation's civil service, business, and scientific enterprises.

The high culture of the particular society: Traditional Oxford and Cambridge (before 1850). These institutions served only a small proportion of the population and were designed to preserve an elitist high culture in a strongly class-based society.

The established morality of the society: Catholic, Muslim, Confucian, and Protestant colleges and universities.[17] The Jesuit universities around the world, following the precepts of St. Ignatius; the great House of Wisdom in Baghdad in the Middle Ages; and the Protestant colleges of Holland, Scotland, and the United States that derived from John Calvin's University of Geneva, all took the dissemination of ethical and religious beliefs as their basis of teaching and learning.

The transformation of society: Revolutionary instruction and activities before "the Revolution." The "primary function of Marxists in the university [is to] take part in what is, in fact, a class struggle."[18]

*Illustrative Multiple Assignments
for the Plural-University*

Ortega: Professional training, research, training for leadership, preparation for guiding one's own life

Napoleonic universities: Professional training and culture of the nation

U.S.S.R. (when there was a monolithic U.S.S.R.): Political ideology and technocratic competence.

Illustrative Open-Ended Assignments
for all of Higher Education,
Including the Multiversity

Modern American higher education: "Liberal education," professional training, research, remedial instruction, service to society in many forms, equality of opportunity through education, and creation of "a nation of educated people,"[19] among others. Thus, "any person, any study."[20]

The reports of the Carnegie Commission and the Carnegie Council.[21]

The long-run trends have been (1) from *the* university to diversified institutions of higher education, (2) from one to a few to many assignments, and (3) from service to a few, to many, to most people. Ortega, fifty years ago, stood partway in each of these transitions. He sensed that a unified university by itself was not enough (thus research laboratories on the periphery). He suggested several missions and knew that they were not all compatible with each other. He worried about the education of, but suggested nothing for, the masses.

Ortega's most important new thought was also an old thought-tracing back to the great philosophers of ancient Greece and that was the need to prepare university students to confront the great ideas and the great issues of their age for the sake both of leadership to society and the management of their own lives.

Clark Kerr

Notes

[1]All quotations are from *Mission of the University* unless otherwise noted.

[2]Andrew Dobson concludes that, while Ortega's public silence "was intended to be an eloquent attempt to express his dissatisfaction with both sides" (p. 6), his sympathies gradually came to be more on the side of a "Nationalist victory" (p. 36). (*An Introduction to the Politics and Philosophy of Jose Ortega y Gasset*, [Cambridge: Cambridge University Press, 1989].) Robert McClintock (*Man and His Circumstances: Ortega as Educator* [New York: Columbia Teachers College Press, 1971]) has another explanation that Ortega began withdrawing from politics as early as 1932 full of disappointments (see the discussion in chap. 8 entitled "Failure").

[3]In *The Revolt of the Masses* (authorized translation from the Spanish; New York: W. W. Norton, 1932 [originally published as *La Rebelion de las Masas*, 1930]) he wrote of "the coming of the masses" who are unable to "rule society" but are intent on doing so. This was ushering in "the brutal empire of the masses" whose "intervention is solely by violence." "Mass man" has no "moral code." One consequence was the rise of the "primitivism" of both "Bolshevism" and "Fascism" (pp. 11, 68, 92, 187).

[4]Christian Ceplecha, *The Historical Thought of Jose Ortega y Gasset* (Washington, D.C.: The Catholic University of America Press, 1958), p. 21.

[5]*Ibid.*, p. 95.

[6]"To the Reader," *Meditations on Quixote*, with Introduction and Notes by Julian Marais, translated from the Spanish by Evelyn Rugg and Diego Marin. New York: W. W. Norton & Co., 1961, p. 45. (Originally published 1914.)

[7]Ortega y Gasset's "To the Reader," p. 41.

[8]Compare this listing with that of the Study Commission on Global Commission on Global Education, which recently identified four basic themes for educational programs as including (1) analyses of the world as a series of interrelated systems as identified by Kenneth Boulding (*The World as a Total System* [Beverly Hills: Sage Publications, 1985]) as including the physical system, the biological system, the economic systems, the political systems, and the communication and evaluative systems; (2) perspectives on the historical development of modern civilizations; (3) intercultural understanding; and (4) preparation of citizens to make public policy (*The United States Prepares for Its Future: Global Perspectives in Education*, Report of the Study Commission on Global Education, Clark Kerr, Chair [New York: Global Perspectives in Education, 1987]), pp. 17-22). This is my own single favorite selection of a "great theme" for the current age: The movement toward a more nearly world society.

[9]Ceplecha, *Historical Thought of Jose Ortega y Gasset*, p. 121.

[10]Ibid., p. 125.

[11]See the proposal in The Carnegie Foundation for the Advancement of Teaching, *Missions of the College Curriculum* (San Francisco: Jossey-Bass, 1977), p. 13; and Carnegie Commission on Higher Education, *Reform on Campus* (New York: McGraw-Hill, 1972), p. 41ff. Ortega's proposal does involve a "broad learning experience" but with this important qualification: that it be oriented toward the future.

[12]Some of them, of course, are great ideas for the current age as well. And this category can additionally be broken down into (a) ideas in one's own civilization and (b) great ideas from other civilizations.

[13]Robert Maynard Hutchins, *The Higher Learning in America* (New Haven: Yale University Press, 1936); and *The Learning Society* (New York: Frederick A. Praeger, Publishers, 1968).

[14]Cardinal John Henry Newman, *The Idea of a University* (New York and London: Longings, Green & Co., 1927 [originally published 1852]).

[15]Abraham Flexner, *Universities: American, English, German* (New York: Oxford University Press, 1930); and Abraham Flexner, *Medical Education in the United States and Canada: A Report to The Carnegie Foundation for the Advancement of Teaching* (New York: Arno Press, 1972 [originally published in 1910 as *Bulletin of The Carnegie Foundation for the Advancement of Teaching*, no. 4]).

[16]Benjamin Franklin, *Proposals Relating to Education of Youth in Pennsylvania* (Philadelphia, 1749).

[17]Harvard College was established, said its founders, "to advance *Learning* and perpetuate it to Posterity; dreading to leave an illiterate Ministery to the Churches, when our present Ministers shall lie in the Dust."

[18]Richard Lewontin, "Marxists and the University," *New Political Science* 1 (Fall-Winter 1979-80): p. 25-30.

[19]See Howard R. Bowen, *The State of the Nation and the Agenda for Higher Education* (San Francisco: Jossey-Bass, 1982), pp. 101-102.

[20]Eric Ashby, *Any Person, Any Study: An Essay on Higher Education in the United States* (New York: McGraw-Hill, 1971). Ashby took the title of his book from Ezra Cornell's remark that he "would found an institution in which any person can find instruction in any study."

[21]See in particular Carnegie Commission of Higher Education, *The Purposes and the Performance of Higher Education in the United States: Approaching the Year 2000* (New York: McGraw-Hill, 1973), which suggested these five basic functions for American higher education: The provision of opportunities for the intellectual, aesthetic, ethical, and skill development of individual students, and the provision of campus environments that can constructively assist students in their more general developmental growth; the advancement of human capability in society at large; the enlargement of educational justice for the postsecondary age group; the transmission and advancement of learning and wisdom; and the critical evaluation of society-through individual thought and persuasion—for the sake of society's self-renewal. Also see Carnegie Council on Policy Studies in Higher Education, *Giving Youth a Better Chance: Options for Education, Work and Service* (San Francisco: Jossey-Bass, 1979), which suggested these roles for community colleges: developing training and work-experience programs in conjunction with government agencies; experimenting with admitting students at age sixteen and developing "middle college" encompassing the last year of traditional high school; providing opportunities for high school students to participate in the colleges' occupational programs; developing more opportunities for cooperative education and apprenticeship programs for both secondary and postsecondary students; and other opportunities—thus accepting a "residual responsibility for youth" (p. 25).

A TEMPERED SPIRIT OF REFORM

CHAPTER I

A Tempered Spirit of Reform

THE Federation of University Students asked me to come here and speak to you on the reform of education.[1] Now I loathe speaking in public, to such an extent that I have managed to do so very few times in my life. Yet this time, without a moment's hesitation, I let myself be corralled by the students. Which shows with what enthusiasm I have come here. In fact, I come with great enthusiasm, but with small faith. For it is clear that these are two different things. Man would be badly off, indeed, if he were incapable of enthusiasm except for the things in which he has faith! Humanity would still be pursuing its existence in a hole in the ground; for everything that has made it possible to emerge from the cave and the primeval jungle appeared in its first hour as a highly dubious undertaking. Nevertheless, man has been able to grow enthusiastic over his vision of these unconvincing enterprises. He has put himself to work for the sake of an idea, seeking by magnificent exertions to arrive at the incredible. And in the end, he has arrived there. Beyond all doubt it is one of the vital sources of man's power, to be thus able to kindle enthusiasm from the mere glimmer of something improbable, difficult, remote. The other sort of enthusiasm, cradled comfortably by faith, is hardly worthy of the name, because it is sure of its success from the outset. Little is to be expected from the man who exerts himself only when

[1] EDITOR'S NOTE: Mrs. Helene Weyl dates this address "late in the autumn, or more likely, in the early winter of 1930." The present book, which was published soon after the lecture, bears the date 1930, and speaks of the *Rebelión de las Masas* as "recientemente publicado." The first edition of the *Rebelión*, though dated 1929, has a colophon stating that the printing was finished August 26, 1930.

3

he has the certainty of being recompensed in the end! I remember having written in 1916 that the Germans would lose
the war, because they had entered it too sure of victory:
their mind was wholly on the conquering, and not simply on
fighting. One must go into any kind of struggle prepared for
anything, including calamity and defeat. For these, as much
as victory, are masks life can put on in a moment. Every day
the conviction forces itself on me with new clarity, that too
much security demoralizes men more than anything else.
Because they came to feel too secure, all the aristocracies of
history have fallen into irreparable degeneracy. And one of
the ailments of the present time, particularly of the rising
generation, is that the modern man, thanks to technological
progress and social organization, is inclined to feel sure of
too many things about his life.[2]

Do not be surprised therefore that I come before you,
according to an old peculiarity of human nature, with more
enthusiasm than faith. But why do I have so little faith? Let
me tell you. It is now close to twenty-five years since I wrote
my first articles on the reform of the Spanish state in general
and the university in particular—articles which won me the
friendship of don Francisco Giner de los Ríos. In those days,
you could count on your fingers all the people in Spain who
admitted the necessity of reforming either the state or the
university. Anyone who dared speak of reform, or even insin-
uate that it was appropriate, was *ipso facto* declared a madman and an outlaw. He was cast off on a tangent from the
circle of normal Spanish society, regardless of who he might
be, and condemned to a marginal existence, as if reform were
leprosy. Do not think that this hostility toward the slightest
suspicion of reform arose because the reformers were a radical lot, a menace to society, etc., etc. Not at all. The most
moderate of men would have been ostracized for the mention

[2] AUTHOR'S NOTE: On this matter see my recent book *The Revolt of
the Masses.*

of reform. Such was the case of Antonio Maura, who had been raised to the height of power by the conservatives themselves. Convinced that even the most conservative point of view required changes in the organization of the state, Maura found himself suddenly relegated to the periphery of the national life. His attempt at reform was crushed by a witticism in vogue at the time, comparing him to a rural policeman in a china shop. Two things escaped the wits who bandied this joke about—one, that in a few years their china shop was to be invaded by the whole police force on horseback; and the other, that they revealed a stubborn determination on their own part to preserve a *status quo* which had about it, indeed, all the frailty of chinaware.

I cite this notorious example to indicate the general, hidebound obstinacy which opposed the reform of anything then in power in Spain, including the state and the university. Those of us who advocated change and proposed to revise antiquated forms were called again and again "enemies of the University." For supporting new institutions like the *Residencia de Estudiantes*, which was created precisely to promote the welfare of the university by stimulating the ferment of thought, we were dubbed the university's official enemies. Today, of course, those who reviled the loudest are just the people who hasten to imitate the *Residencia de Estudiantes*. In this they deserve nothing but praise. But at the same time it is only fair to recall that, for many years, gibes and insults were the portion of those who felt some honest concern for the Spanish university and were determined that it should not continue indefinitely to be the sad, inert, spiritless thing it then was. For candor obliges one to observe that our university today is decidedly different from what it was, though it is still far from what it ought to be, and can be.

At present, throughout all our national life, the constellations have changed. Hard-fisted facts have come to silence the carping mouths and convince the slowest among us that

5

government and university alike need reform: it is not a question of desiring reform or not; it is imperative that we make an effort, because neither of these institutions is working. They are machines worn out by the wear and tear of use and abuse.

Today we are not alone. Many people desire the transformation of the Spanish body politic, and those who do not are resigned to bear with it, somehow or other. Certainly the moment is full of opportunity. You do not appreciate, young people, what good fortune you have had: you have come into life at a magnificent juncture in the destinies of Spain—when the horizon lies open, and many, many great things are going to be possible, among them a new state and a new university. It would be difficult to be more optimistic than I am concerning the interpretation to be put on the current situation of the country. Events which nearly everyone has viewed with alarm seem to me to be ironical masks, under whose evil appearance are hidden really favorable developments. Certainly the moment is full of opportunity; you have come at the dawn of an illustrious era. A people dormant for centuries is beginning to stir, with those sleepy, jerking motions of a person about to awake and rise to his feet. The moment can be happily described by that very expressive line of poetry, in which the venerable poem of the Cid relates the dawning of a day:

Apriessa cantan los gallos e quieren crebrar albores . . .[3]

Then has not the moment arrived for joining a new faith with the old enthusiasm? To this I must answer, provisionally, "No, . . . not yet." In my optimism, it strikes me as clear and definite that the horizon which lies open before the Spaniard of today is a magnificent one. Now the horizon is a symbol of possibilities, presenting themselves before our

[3] "Abruptly, cocks begin to crow, the light of dawn is about to break" (*Poema de mio Cid*, line 235).

6

human life. And this life of ours, in its turn, is a process of converting these possibilities into actual realities. Here is the point where my optimism falters, and my faith fails me. For in history—in life—possibilities do not become realities of their own accord; someone, with his hands and his brain, with his labor and his self-sacrifice, must make realities of them. History and life, for this reason, are a perpetual *creating*. Our life is not given to us ready-made: in a fundamental sense it is, precisely, what we are constantly and continuously making of ourselves. The process is going on at every instant. Nothing is ours outright, as a gift; we have to perform for ourselves even those of our actions which seem most passive. The humble Sancho Panza kept suggesting this on all occasions, by repeating his proverb: "If they give you the cow, you have to carry the rope." All we are given is possibilities—to make ourselves one thing or another. At this instant, for example, you are engaged in listening: decidedly no easy occupation, as you can tell from the fact that if you relax your attention the least bit, your listening will sink into mere hearing; or a bit more, and your fugitive attention would fail to register the boom of a cannon.

I say, then, that the circumstances offer a magnificent opportunity for a thorough reform of the Spanish state and university. But the reform of the one and of the other waits to be done *by someone*. Is there such a one in Spain today? By that I do not mean an individual, of course, one of those mythical creatures usually referred to, by a misapprehension, as a Great Man. History is not made by one man—however great he may be. History is not like a sonnet; nor is it a game of solitaire. It is made by many people: by groups of people endowed, collectively, with the necessary qualities.

Since I have come here today with the intention of talking to you in absolute sincerity; since, out of loyalty to myself, I am resolved to say my say without mincing words, I cannot disguise my grave doubt that there exists, on this day, any group capable of achieving the reform of the state, or to limit ourselves to the present theme, the reform of the university. I say on this day—this fleeting day on which I am speaking. Within a dozen days, or weeks, this group *can* exist and I hope it will. Nothing prevents it from being brought together and organized: if I stress so emphatically that we lack such a group today, it is with the sole purpose of contributing to its realization tomorrow.

But you will say: "How can you doubt that a group exists, capable of effecting the reform? Once it is admitted that a thing is feasible, all that is necessary is the will to do it. And here are we, fairly clamoring for the reform of the university. There can be no doubt whether the group exists."

Certainly, certainly. To accomplish a thing which is possible, all you need is the will to do it. But everything depends on how fully the sense of this easy word is understood. It is easy to say and even to think that you are resolved upon something; but it is extremely difficult to be resolved in the true sense.

For this means resolving upon all the things which are necessary as intermediate steps; its means, for one thing, providing ourselves with the qualities that are requisite for the undertaking. Anything short of this is no real resolution, it is simply wishing. You rinse your imagination in the idea, you work yourself into a voluptuous excitement over it, and you spend your force in a vague effervescence of enthusiasm. In his *Philosophy of Universal History*, Hegel asserts that passion, without doubt, is responsible for all the significant accomplishments in history; but—he qualifies—*cool passion*. When passion is simply a frenzy of turbulent emotion, it is of no use at all. Anyone could be passionate, that way. But it is not so easy to maintain that sort of fire which is both critical and creative, that incandescence so supplied with thermal energy that it will not be cooled when the two coldest things in the world come to lodge within it: cool logic and an iron will. The vulgar, false, impotent sort of passion shrinks in terror from the proximity of reflective thought, for it senses that at such a chilly contact it will be frozen out of existence. Hence the symptom of high creative passion is that it seeks to complete itself by uniting with the cooler virtues; that it admits of reflective criticism, without losing its creative energy. It is fire supported with the constancy of clear understanding and a calm will.

This kind of resolute, clear-seeing will is what I do not find today, even at a formative stage, in any group of Spaniards—including yourselves. And without it, we shall await in vain the execution of a reform, a work of construction and creation.

The root of Spain's troubles, whether in the state or the university, may be given the most various names; but if you seek the very tip of the root, out of which all the rest arises and emerges, you encounter a fact which only one word can adequately describe: slovenliness.[4] It penetrates our whole national life from top to bottom, directing, inspiring its actions. The state is slovenly in its dealings with the citizen, permitting him, on occasion, to evade compliance with its laws; or vice versa, the state itself applies the laws fraudulently and makes them a means of deceiving the citizen. Some day the story will be told, for instance, of what the government did on the authority of that famous law passed during the emergencies of the World War, called the "Law of Subsistencies." Things you would consider a far cry from any question of subsistence were perpetrated under the title of this law. Everyone knows what use the governors of provinces have made, for decades, of the Law of Associations. Just ask about that for yourselves, among the labor unions in the provinces. But it is not my intention now to present pathetic cases of this shabby deportment of the state. I am

[4] EDITOR'S NOTE: One would like a slightly milder word to render *la chabacanería.*

not here to talk politics, and moreover if I were, I should not be pathetic about it. My purpose is to make clear to you what constitutes this fundamental ailment of Spain and the Spaniard, which I call slovenliness. For there is no use to rant and declaim, after the fashion of public orations, that this conduct of the government is a crime, an intolerable abuse, a betrayal of public trust. It is all that, of course; but so meanly, so stupidly, so habitually—so far from any compensating profit to the government—that one feels ashamed to call it crime. To tell the truth, while it is crime in the juridical sense, it is not crime as a psychological fact—as a historical reality. Crime is something violent and terrible, and in this regard, respectable: this is no crime, but something inferior to crime. It is, in a word, slovenliness, the lack of all decorum, of all self-respect, of all decency in the state's manner of performing its peculiarly delicate function.

I do not mean by this that in Spain crimes are not committed. But I do deny that crimes are the bulk, or the worst, of Spain's trouble. For crimes, when they are really that, provoke a reaction, before very long, to cure the ailment. Slovenliness on the contrary grows accustomed to its own presence; it finds itself pleasantly comfortable, and tends to spread and perpetuate itself. Thus it permeates everything in Spain, from the state and its official acts, to the life of the family and the very grimace of the individual. In our university faculty meetings, the atmosphere is heavy with this slovenliness; and to walk through these halls, even on ordinary days, and hear the hullabaloo and see the gesticulations of you students, is to breathe an atmosphere so thick with slovenliness that it chokes.[5]

But the full meaning of a concept never becomes clear

[5] AUTHOR'S NOTE: For a number of years I have had to find a room outside the university buildings, because the habitual shouting of our precious students, standing around in the halls, makes it impossible to hear oneself talk in the classrooms.

until it is confronted with its opposite, as for example up and down, more and less, etc. Every idea has its antagonist; in the combat between the two, their profile is delineated. What is the opposite of slovenliness? I shall use a word with which you are very familiar, since it belongs to the vocabulary of sports. The opposite of slovenliness is *to be in form*. You people well know the tremendous difference there is between an athlete when he is *in form*, and the same man when he is out of form. The difference in what he is able to do is every bit as striking as if he were two entirely different people. But this *form* is a thing that has to be acquired. In order to achieve it, the individual must first go off by himself and concentrate upon his own development: he has to go into training, and give up many things, in the determination to surpass himself, to be more alert, tense, supple. There is nothing that is indifferent to him, for every little thing either is favorable to his form, or else pulls it down, and with this in mind he goes out for one thing and avoids the other. Briefly, to be in form means never indulging in any dissipation whatever. And that indulgence of oneself—your "let it go anyhow," "it's all the same," "a bit more or less," "what of it?"—that is slovenliness.

Just as individuals, groups too may be in form or out of form, and it is evident in history that the only groups which have ever done anything are those which have achieved *form*: compact, perfectly organized groups, in which every member knows that the others will not fail him at the crucial point, so that the whole body may move swiftly in any direction without losing its balance or losing its head—as the abbé Fernando Galiani said of the Order of the Jesuits in the eighteenth century, when that Order was in form, "It is a sword with its hilt in Rome and its point everywhere." But a group does not acquire this *form* unless it has disciplined itself, and continues to discipline itself; unless it sees with perfect clarity what it proposes to do. And it cannot see clearly unless the purpose it sees is clear, well thought out, cogent, and as complete as the situation warrants.

All this is what I was referring to earlier. I doubt, then, that there exists in Spain, at the present moment, a group which is *in form* for the reforming of the state or of the university. And if it is not *in form*, all that may be attempted without the necessary qualities will come to nothing. It is obvious, in as much as slovenliness is the root of the evil, that a reform which is slovenly itself will not mend matters appreciably. You have seen for yourselves a petulant effort to reform the country, on the part of a group of people who had not given a moment's thought to the question of first providing themselves with the minimum of necessary equipment. Such has been the Dictatorship.[6] All it has achieved, despite the extraordinary opportunity that offered itself, has been to carry our national slovenliness to the point of madness.

Let it be understood that I have not come here to advise you against taking part in the public affairs of Spain, or against petitioning, and even insisting upon, the reform of the university. On the contrary: I urge you to do all this; but do it seriously—do it *in form*. Otherwise, the future can be told now, with perfect assurance. If you attempt to take a part in public life without the proper preparation, this is what will happen. Since activity in public affairs means trying to influence the great mass of the public, and you are not a powerful, articulated body but merely a little formless mass, then the mechanics of history, identical at this point with the laws of physics, will simply follow its inexorable course. The larger mass will crush the smaller.

To exert influence upon a mass, you must be something other than a mass yourselves: a live force, or in other words, a group *in form*.

---

[6] EDITOR'S NOTE: The dictatorship had begun under Primo de Rivera in 1923, and was to last until the establishment of the Republic in 1931.

If I could see in you the determination to put yourselves in form—ah!—then, my friends, I should not be afflicted with this deficiency of faith.

I should believe it all to be possible, indeed, imminent. Contrary to a general belief, history may advance by jumps, and not always by gradual change. It was the characteristic error of the past century to count upon gradual evolution, and to presume that every whole achievement in history was produced by means of a very gradual preparation. It was a surprise when facts showed, clearly and undeniably, that in biology and in the spiritual world alike, spontaneous realities could emerge suddenly and in a sense without preparation.

To cite a symbolic case, let me recall to you how stupefied the historians were in the last century, when the fact was established that the highest, classical civilization of the Egyptians—the marvelous culture of the Pyramids—was without predecessors. It caused great astonishment to find that this most exquisite flourishing in the whole course of the Nile valley civilization appeared at the threshold of history—at the dawn of historic times. It had been supposed that excavation would reveal, under the land of the Pyramids, some vestiges of a less perfect culture, in progress toward that mature perfection. Great was the surprise when the archaeologists struck the remains, almost immediately under the pyramids, of a neolithic civilization. Which is to say that almost without transition, man had advanced from the chipped stone to the classic stone.[7]

No; history proceeds very often by jumps. These jumps, in which tremendous distances may be covered, are called generations. A generation *in form* can accomplish what centuries failed to achieve without form. And there, my young friends, lies a challenge.

[7] EDITOR'S NOTE: Though later evidence indicates a longer and more significant epoch of transition, the case still illustrates the possibility of rapid social evolution.

THE FUNDAMENTAL QUESTION

CHAPTER II

The Fundamental Question

[1]THE reform of higher education cannot be limited, nor can even its main features be limited, to the correction of abuses. Reform is always the creation of new usages. Abuses are always of minor importance. For either they are abuses in the most natural sense of the word, namely, isolated, infrequent cases of departure from usage; or else they are so frequent and customary, so persistent and so generally tolerated, that they are no longer to be called abuses. In the first case, they will presumably be corrected automatically; in the second case, it would be futile to correct them, for their frequency and acceptance indicate that they are not exceptions to a rule, but manifestations of usages which are bad. It is something in the usage, the policy, and not the breach of it, which needs our attention.

Any reform movement which is limited to correcting slovenly or slipshod abuses in our university will lead inevitably to a reform which is equally slovenly.

What matters is usage. I can go further: a clear symptom that the usages constituting an institution are sound is the ability to withstand a good dose of abuses without serious harm, as a healthy man bears up under stress that would break a weakling. But an institution cannot be built of wholesome usage, until its precise mission has been determined. An institution is a machine in that its whole structure and functioning must be devised in view of the service it is

[1] EDITOR'S NOTE: The first three paragraphs of Chapter II have here been omitted. In them Ortega recapitulates Chapter I, and complains of the hall in which he had read that chapter. This is the only omission made in the present translation.

expected to perform. In other words, the root of university reform is a complete formulation of its purpose. Any alteration, or touching up, or adjustment about this house of ours, unless it starts by reviewing the problem of its mission—clearly, decisively, truthfully—will be love's labors lost.

Through their failure to do this, all the improvements attempted hitherto, motivated in some cases by excellent intentions, including the projects worked out some years ago by the university faculty itself, have inevitably come to nought. They will never achieve the one thing which is both sufficient and requisite for any being—individual or collective—to live to the full of its powers: namely, that its life be the true, authentic fulfillment of its powers, and not some falsification of this inexorable destiny, imposed upon it by our stubborn and arbitrary preferences. The best attempts of the last fifteen years—not to speak of the worst—instead of putting the question squarely, "What is a university for, and what must it consequently be?" have done the thing that was easiest and most sterile. They have looked about to see what is done in the universities of other peoples.

I do not criticize our informing ourselves by observing an exemplary neighbor; on the contrary, that is necessary. But such observation cannot excuse us from the labor of determining our destiny for ourselves. By this I do not mean any quest after "racial purity" and all that nonsense. Even if we were all—men or nations—identical with one another, imitation would still be fatal. For in imitating, we evade that creative exertion of laboring at a problem, from which we can learn the real nature, including the limits and the defects, of the solution we borrow. There is no question here of "racial purity," which is, in Spain anyway, as common as the hayseeds. It is immaterial whether we come to the same conclusions and the same forms as other countries; what matters is that we arrive by our own legs, after a personal combat with the fundamental question at issue.

The reasoning of our best attempts so far has been fallacious: British life has been, and is, a marvel; *therefore* the British secondary schools must be exemplary, *since* out of them British life has grown. German science is prodigious; therefore the German university is a model institution, *because* it engendered the prodigy. So let us imitate the British secondary schools and the German higher education.

The error stems directly from the nineteenth century as a whole. The English rout Napoleon I: "The battle of Waterloo was won on the playing fields of Eton." Bismarck crushes Napoleon III: "The war of 1870 is the victory of the Prussian schoolmaster and the German professor."

These clichés rest upon a fundamental error which we shall simply have to get out of our heads. It consists in supposing that nations are great *because* their schools are good —elementary, secondary, or higher. It is the residue of a pious "idealism" of the past century. It ascribes to the school a force which it neither has nor can have. That century, in order to feel enthusiasm for a thing, or even just to esteem it especially, found it necessary to exaggerate the thing to heroic proportions. Certainly *when* a nation is great, so will be its schools. There is no great nation without great schools. But the same holds for its religion, its statesmanship, its economy, and a thousand other things. A nation's greatness is the integration of many elements. If a people is bad politically, it is vain to expect anything at all of the most perfect school system. In such a case schools are for the few, who live apart and estranged from the rest of the country. Perhaps some day these educated few may influence the collective life of their country, and succeed in improving the whole national school system.

Principle of education: the school, when it is truly a functional organ of the nation, depends far more on the atmosphere of national culture in which it is immersed than it does on the pedagogical atmosphere created artificially within it. A condition of equilibrium between this inward and outward pressure is essential to produce a good school.

Consequence: even granting that English secondary education and German higher education are perfect, they would not be transferable, for the institutions are only a part of a larger entity. Their being, in its totality, is nothing less than the whole nation which created and maintains them.

Furthermore, the short-circuited reasoning I have described prevented its victims from looking squarely at these model schools and seeing what they are within themselves, purely as institutional structures. The framework was confused with the ambient air of English life, or German thought. Now in as much as neither English life nor German thought can be transported here but, at best, only the disengaged institutional structures, it is quite important that we see what these actually are, apart from those virtues which enveloped and pervaded them in their native countries.

Then one sees that the German university is, as an institution, a rather deplorable object. If German science had been dependent for its nourishment on the forces of the university, as an institution, that science would be of very small account. Fortunately an atmosphere of free inquiry has combined with the German's natural talent and disposition for science to outweigh the glaring imperfections of the German university. I am not well acquainted with English secondary education; but what I can discern of it leads me to think that there too the institutional structure is very defective.

But there is no need of my personal opinions. It is a fact, that secondary education in England and the university in Germany are undergoing a crisis. Fundamental criticism of the latter by the first Prussian Minister of Education since the founding of the Republic: Becker. The discussion which has ensued.[2]

[2] EDITOR'S NOTE: See p. 44 and note. For the explanation of Ortega's unfinished sentences see his dedication, p. 9.

Because they have been willing to imitate and to evade thinking through the questions for themselves, our best professors live in all respects in a spirit fifteen or twenty years behind the times, except that they are up to date in the details of their fields. And this is the tragic lag behindhand, which is the fate of people who try to save themselves the effort of being authentic and forming their own convictions. The number of years comprising this lag is not a matter of chance. All the creation of history—in science, in politics—arises out of a certain pervading state of mind, or "spirit of the times." This state of mind changes at rhythmic intervals: the interval of the generation.[3] Out of the spirit of a generation come ideas, evaluations, and so on. The person who imitates these must wait until they have been formulated; or in other words, until the preceding generation has finished its work. Then he adopts its principles, at the time when they are beginning to decline, and a new generation is already making its reform, inaugurating the regime of a new spirit. Each generation struggles for fifteen years to establish itself, and its synthesis holds together another fifteen years—inevitable anachronism of an imitative, unauthentic people.

Let us look abroad for information. But not for a model.

There is no evading the fundamental question, then: What is the mission of the university?

[3] EDITOR'S NOTE: Ortega has elaborated "The Concept of the Generation" in *The Modern Theme*, Chapter I and ff. For the background of the concept, see the résumé and brief bibliography in Christian Sénéchal, *Les grands courants de la littérature française contemporaine*, Paris: Malfère (1933), pp. 419-421; the introduction of Bopp and Paulhan to Albert Thibaudet, *Histoire de la littérature française de 1789 à nos jours*, Paris: Stock (1937); and also Sainte-Beuve's observation concerning individual literary production, in *Nouveaux lundis*, III, art. "Chateaubriand," part II (1862): "Quinze ans d'ordinaire font une carrière; il est donné à quelques-uns de la doubler, d'en recommencer ou même d'en remplir une seconde."

21

To determine what the mission of the university is, let us try first to define what the university actually means today, in Spain and elsewhere. Whatever may be the differences in status, all the universities of Europe have some general characteristics in common.[4]

[4] AUTHOR'S NOTE: It is usual, for example, to exaggerate the differences between the English and continental universities, neglecting the fact that the greatest differences are to be laid not to the universities themselves, but to the very extraordinary English character. What should be compared between countries is the tendencies which mark the evolution of their universities—not the degree, naturally variable, in which the tendencies have progressed. Thus, the conservatism of the English has caused them to maintain appearances, in their higher institutions, which they recognize themselves to be irrelevant, and which, indeed, they value as mere fictions quite incidental to the vital reality of British university life. It would seem ridiculous for someone to presume to limit the free will of the Englishman, and censure him for indulging, if he could and wanted to, in the luxury of consciously perpetuating these fictions. But it would be just as naive to take these figments seriously, and suppose that the Englishman deludes himself about their fictitious character. The studies I have read on the English university fall invariably into the subtle snare of English irony. They fail to notice that if England preserves the nonprofessional *aspect* of the university, like the wig of the magistrate, it is not through any obstinate belief that these are actualities, but precisely *because* they are antiquated and superfluous. Otherwise they could not provide the luxury, the diversion, the occasion for awe, and other values which the Englishman seeks in these mere appearances. Beneath the quaint peruke, the justice is modern to the minute; and beneath its nonprofessional aspect, the English university has become, in the last forty years, as professionalized as any other.

It is likewise not of the slightest importance for our central theme—the mission of the university—that the English universities are not institutions of the state. While this fact is of great importance for the life and history of the English people, it does not prevent their university from functioning essentially in the same way as the state-maintained universities of the continent. In the last analysis it would turn out that even in England the universities are institutions of the state; only the Englishman has an entirely different conception of the state from the continental idea of it. To sum up the point I wish to make: first, the enormous differences which exist between the universities of the various nations are not so much concerned with the universities proper as with the nations themselves; and second, the most striking

We meet the fact, first of all, that the university is the institution in which higher education is imparted to almost all those who receive any. "Almost," because there are also the specialized schools, whose separate existence gives rise to a problem likewise separate. Having made this exception, we may lay it aside and work with the practical generalization, that the people who receive higher education receive it in the university. But then we find ourselves face to face with another limitation more important than that of the specialized schools. All those who receive higher education are not all those who could and should receive it; they are only the children of the well-to-do classes. The university represents a privilege difficult to justify or defend. Theme: the working class in the university—a theme as yet intact. For two reasons. First, if one believes it is right, as I do, to offer the knowledge of the university to the working man, it is because one considers this knowledge valuable and desirable. The problem of universalizing the university rests upon the previous determination of what the higher learning and instruction are to be. And second, the process of making the university accessible to the working man is only in small part the concern of the university; it is almost wholly the business of the state. Only a great reform of our state will make our university effective. Failure of all the attempts made so far, such as "university extension," etc.[5]

fact in the last forty years is a convergent movement of all the universities of Europe that is tending to make them all homogeneous.

[5] EDITOR'S NOTE: It should be noted that after half a century of growth, university extension in the United States has become an important agency for the training of people who must meanwhile earn their living. The cultural education of the working man is still admittedly deficient; but this is due rather to our poor understanding of the objective than to a lack of well-intentioned agencies. Organizations and institutions interested in the education of the working man are too numerous to need mention. Among the oldest are the British "Workers

The important thing at this point is to bear well in mind that all the people who receive higher education receive it in the university. If a greater number should receive it tomorrow than at present, so much the better for the force of the argument which follows.

Of what does this higher instruction consist, which is offered in the university to the vast legion of youth? It consists of two things:

(A) The teaching of the learned professions.

(B) Scientific research and the preparation of future investigators.

The university teaches people to be doctors, pharmacists, lawyers, judges, economists, public servants, teachers of the sciences and the humanities in secondary schools, and so on.

In the second place, science itself is cultivated in the university, through research and the transmission of its methods. In Spain, this function of creative science, and of creating scientists, is at a minimum; not by reason of any defect of the university, nor because the university considers that such activities are not its mission, but on account of the notorious lack of scientific callings and aptitude for research which marks our race. No doubt if science were abundantly carried on in Spain, it would be in the university by preference, as is more or less the case in the other countries. Let this point serve as an example, and save us the repetition of the same principle at every step: the obstinate backwardness of Spain in intellectual activity entails the result that we find here in a state of germination or mere tendency what appears elsewhere in its full development. For the purpose of stating the university problem in its basic form, these differences of degree are immaterial. It is sufficient that all the reforms of recent years clearly evince the intention to increase the re-

Educational Association," and Ruskin College in Oxford (founded 1899). For the explanation of Ortega's unfinished sentences see his dedication, p. 9.

search activities of our universities and the training of scientists: in short, to orient the entire institution in this direction. Commonplace and deceptive objections may be advanced on the other side. It is, however, notorious that our best professors, those who have the most influence in the course of the attempted reforms, believe that our university should vie with the foreign universities. And that is enough.

The higher education consists, then, of professionalism and research. Without attacking the subject now, let us note in passing that it is surprising to find two such disparate tasks joined, fused together. For there can be no doubt about this: to be a lawyer, a judge, a doctor, a druggist, a teacher of Latin or history in a secondary school, is very different from being a jurist, a physiologist, a biochemist, a philologist, etc. The former are engaged in practical professions; the latter in purely scientific occupations. Furthermore, society needs many doctors, pharmacists, teachers; but it needs only a restricted number of scientists.[6] If we really needed many of these it would be a catastrophe, since a true calling for science is extremely rare. It is surprising, then, to find mixed together the professional instruction which is for all, and research which is for a very few. But let us put this matter aside for a few moments. Is the higher education nothing more than professionalism and research? At first sight we discover nothing else. But, if we scrutinize the programs of instruction more closely, we discover that the student is nearly always required, apart from his professional apprenticeship and his research, to take some courses of a general character—philosophy, history.

It takes no great acumen to recognize in this requirement the last, miserable residue of something more imposing and

[6] AUTHOR'S NOTE: This number needs to be greater than has been attained at present; but even so, incomparably smaller than the number in the other professions.

25

more meaningful. The symptom that something is a residue—whether in biology or in history—is that we do not perceive why it is with us. In its present form, it serves no end at all; one must trace it back to some other age of its evolution in order to find whole and active what exists today only as a residual stump.[7] The justification which is advanced today, in support of that ancient precept of higher education, is rather vague. The student ought, it is said, to receive something of "general culture."

"General culture." The absurdity of the term, its Philistinism, betrays its insincerity. "Culture," referring to the human mind and not to stock or crops, cannot be anything else but general. There is no being "cultured" in physics or mathematics. That would mean simply to be *learned* in a particular subject. The usage of the expression "general culture" shows an underlying notion that the student ought to be given some ornamental knowledge, which in some way is to educate his moral character or his intellect. For so vague a purpose, one discipline is as good as another, among those that are more or less indefinite and not so technical—like philosophy, or history, or sociology!

But the fact is that if we go back to the medieval epoch in which the university was created, we see clearly that the relic before us is the humble remains of what then constituted higher education, proper and entire.

[7] AUTHOR'S NOTE: Imagine for a moment the conditions of primitive life. One of its constant characteristics is the lack of personal security. It is perilous for two persons to approach each other, for everyone goes about armed. Hence this act has to be safeguarded by customs and ceremonies which give assurance that weapons have been left behind, and that the hand is not going to reach suddenly for one that is hidden. For this purpose, the best procedure is for each man, upon approaching, to grasp the hand of the other—the killing hand, which is normally the right hand. Such is the origin and purpose of our salute by shaking hands, which in the present times, remote from that type of life, is an incomprehensible relic.

The medieval university does no research.[8] It is very little concerned with professions. All is *general culture*—theology, philosophy, "arts."[9]

But what is called "general culture" today was something very different for the Middle Ages. It was not an ornament for the mind or a training of the character. It was, on the contrary, the system of ideas, concerning the world and humanity, which the man of that time possessed. It was, consequently, the repertory of convictions which became the effective guide of his existence.

Life is a chaos, a tangled and confused jungle in which man is lost. But his mind reacts against the sensation of bewilderment: he labors to find "roads," "ways" through the woods,[10] in the form of clear, firm ideas concerning the universe, positive convictions about the nature of things. The ensemble, or system, of these ideas, is culture in the true sense of the term; it is precisely the opposite of external ornament. Culture is what saves human life from being a mere disaster; it is what enables man to live a life which is something above meaningless tragedy or inward disgrace.

We cannot live on the human level without ideas. Upon them depends what we do. Living is nothing more nor less than doing one thing instead of another. Hence the oldest book of India: "Our acts follow our thoughts as the wheel of the cart follows the hoof of the ox." In this sense—which by itself implies no intellectualistic doctrine[11]—we *are* our ideas.

[8] AUTHOR's NOTE: Which does not mean that no research was done in the Middle Ages.

[9] EDITOR's NOTE: The exaggeration here does not essentially damage Sr. Ortega's thesis that the modern university should teach a kind of "culture" which this reference to the Middle Ages helps to describe.

[10] AUTHOR's NOTE: Whence there arises at the beginning of all cultures a term expressing "road" in this sense: the *odos* and *methodos* of the Greeks, the *tao* and *te* of the Chinese, the *path* and *vehicle* of India.

[11] AUTHOR's NOTE: Our ideas or convictions may well be unintellectualistic, as mine are, and in general, the ideas of our age.

Gideon, in this case exceptionally profound, would make it clear that man is always born into a specific period. That is, he is called to live his life at some definite stage in the unfolding of human destinies. A man belongs to a generation; he is of one substance with it. And each generation takes its place not in some chance location, but directly and squarely upon the preceding one. This comes to mean that man lives, perforce, at *the level of his time*,[12] and more particularly, at *the level of the ideas of his time*.

Culture is the *vital* system of ideas of a period. It makes not a particle of difference whether these ideas, or convictions, lie partly or wholly in the province of science. Culture is not science. It is characteristic of our present culture that a great part of its content proceeds out of science; but in other cultures this has not been the case, nor is it decreed anywhere that in ours it will always be so to the same degree as at present.

Compared with the medieval university, the contemporary university has developed the mere seed of professional instruction into an enormous activity; it has added the function of research; and it has abandoned almost entirely the teaching or transmission of culture.

It is evident that the change has been pernicious. Europe today is taking its sinister consequences. The convulsive situation in Europe at the present moment is due to the fact that the average Englishman, the average Frenchman, the average German are *uncultured*: they are ignorant of the essential system of ideas concerning the world and man, which belong to our time. This average person is the new barbarian, a laggard behind the contemporary civilization archaic and primitive in contrast with his problems, which are grimly, relentlessly modern.[13] This new barbarian is

[12] AUTHOR'S NOTE: For the concept of "the height of the times," see *The Revolt of the Masses.*

[13] AUTHOR'S NOTE: The analysis of this serious situation is presented in *The Revolt of the Masses.*

above all the professional man, more learned than ever before, but at the same time more uncultured—the engineer, the physician, the lawyer, the scientist.

The blame for this unpredicted barbarity, this radical and tragic anachronism, rests primarily with the pretentious nineteenth-century university of all countries. If this institution should by chance be torn to bits in the frenzy of a barbarous revolution, it would not have the feeblest reason to complain. When one has examined the matter, he must needs come to the conclusion that the guilt of the universities is not compensated for by the prodigious and brilliant service which they have undeniably rendered to science. Let us not be the dupes of science. For if science is the grandest creation of man, it is made possible, after all, by human life. A crime perpetrated against the fundamental conditions of human life cannot be atoned for through science.

The harm is so ingrained that I shall barely be understood by the generation anterior to the one I am addressing.

In the book of a Chinese thinker who lived in the fourth century B.C., Chuang-tsu, certain symbolic characters are conversing together, and one of them, called the God of the Northern Sea, asks, "How shall I talk of the sea to the frog, if he has never left his pond? How shall I talk of the frost to the bird of the summer land, if it has never left the land of its birth? How shall I talk of life with the sage, if he is the prisoner of his doctrine?"

Society needs good professional men—judges, doctors, engineers—and therefore the university is prepared to furnish professional training. But society needs before this, and more than this, to be assured that the capacity is developed for another kind of profession, the profession of governing. In every society someone governs, whether a group or a class, few people or many. By "governing" I mean not so much the legal exercise of authority as a diffuse pressure, or influence, exerted upon the body politic. Today, the societies in Europe are governed by the bourgeois classes, whose majority is composed of professional men. It is of the first importance to these societies, therefore, that these professional people, aside from their several professions, possess the power to make their lives a vital influence, in harmony with the height of their times. Hence it is imperative to set up once more, in the university, the teaching of the culture, the system of vital ideas, which the age has attained. This is the basic function of the university. This is what the university must be, above all else.

If the working man should become the governing man tomorrow, the problem remains the same: he must govern in accordance with the height of the times—otherwise his regime will be supplanted.[14]

When one considers that the European countries have deemed it admissible to grant professional titles and prestige to magistrates and doctors without making sure that these men have a clear idea, for example, of the physical conception we now have of the world, and an equally clear idea of the character and limitations of the marvelous science by which that concept has been attained—we need not be surprised that affairs have come to such a pass in Europe. At a juncture like this, let us not bandy about fine phrases. The vague desire for a vague culture, I repeat, will lead us nowhere. Physics, and its method, is one of the great essential instruments of the modern mind. Into that science have gone four centuries of intellectual discipline, and its doctrine is intimately connected with the cultured man's concept of God and society, of matter and that which is not matter, together with all the other essentials for an enlightened life. Of course, one can do without that science and be neither

[14] AUTHOR'S NOTE: Since in actual practice the working man does govern, sharing that function with the middle class, it is urgent that the university education be extended to him.

disgraced nor condemned—in certain situations: if one is a humble shepherd in the hills, or a serf attached to the soil, or a manual laborer enslaved to the machine. But the gentleman who professes to be a doctor, or magistrate, or general, or philologist, or bishop—that is, a person who belongs to the directive class of society—if he is ignorant of what the physical cosmos is today for the European man, is a perfect barbarian, however well he may know his laws, or his medicines, or his Holy Fathers. And I should say the same of the person who has not a decently coherent picture of the great movements of history which have brought Humanity to its present parting of ways (for ours is a day of crucial situations). And I should say the same again of the person who has no definite idea of how speculative philosophy conceives today its perpetual essay to formulate a plan of the universe; or how biology endeavors to interpret the fundamental facts of organic life.

For the moment, let us not obscure this simple, evident proposition, by raising the question of how a lawyer, without preparation in higher mathematics, can understand the idea of twentieth-century physics. We shall deal with that question later. For now, let us simply admit into our minds, as we must, the light which proceeds from this observation. The man who does not possess the concept of physics (not the science of physics proper, but the vital idea of the world which it has created), and the concept afforded by history and by biology, and the scheme of speculative philosophy, is not an educated man. Unless he should happen to be endowed with exceptional qualities, it is extremely unlikely that such a man will be, in the fullest sense, a good doctor, a good judge, or a good technical expert. But it is certain that all the other things he does in life, including parts of his profession itself which transcend its proper academic boundaries, will turn out unfortunately. His political ideas and actions will be inept; his affairs of the heart, beginning with

31

the type of woman he will prefer, will be crude and ridiculous; he will bring to his family life an atmosphere of unreality and cramped narrowness, which will warp the upbringing of his children; and outside, with his friends, he will emit thoughts that are monstrosities, and opinions that are a torrent of drivel and bluff.

There is no other way: to move with assurance in the tangle of life, one must be cultivated, one must know the topography—the "ways" and "methods." One must have an idea of the time and place in which he lives: in a word, the "culture" of the age. Now then, this culture is either received, or else it is invented. He who exposes himself to the labor of inventing it for himself, accomplishing alone what thirty centuries of humanity have already accomplished, is the only man who has the right to deny the proposition that the university must undertake to impart culture. But the unfortunate truth is that this lone person, who could oppose my thesis, would have to be a madman!

Civilization has had to await the beginning of the twentieth century, to see the astounding spectacle of how brutal, how stupid, and yet how aggressive is the man learned in one thing and fundamentally ignorant of all else.[15] Professionalism and specialism, through insufficient counterbalancing, have smashed the European man in pieces; and he is consequently missing at all the points where he claims to be, and is badly needed. The engineer possesses engineering; but that is just one piece, one dimension of the European man: the whole man is not to be found in this fragment called "engineer." And so in the rest of the cases. When one says that "Europe is broken in pieces," thinking to use a baroque and exaggerated expression, he says more truth than he suspects. Indeed, the crumbling away of Europe which we are witnessing is the result of the invisible

15 AUTHOR's NOTE: See the chapter entitled "The barbarism of specialization" in *The Revolt of the Masses*.

fragmentation that the European man has progressively undergone.[16]

The great task immediately before us is something like a jigsaw puzzle: we have to reassemble out of scattered pieces —*disiecta membra*—a complete living organism, the European man. What we must achieve is that every individual, or (not to be Utopian) many individuals, should each succeed in constituting the type of the whole man in its entirety. What force can bring this about, if it is not the university?

Then there are no two ways about it. The university must add this other function, huge as it is, to the list of those it already attempts to accomplish.

For that matter, outside Spain a movement is making itself felt with great vigor, to orient higher education toward the teaching of culture, or the transmission to the newer generation of the system of ideas concerning the world and man which has reached its maturity with the passing generation.

We come to the conclusion therefore that the university's teaching comprises these three functions:

I. The transmission of culture.
II. The teaching of the professions.
III. Scientific research and the training of new scientists.

Have we thus answered our question, What is the mission of the university? By no means: we have only massed together what the university of today believes to be its business, and one thing which, in our judgment, it is not doing but must do. We have prepared the question; no more than that.

It seems to me unnecessary, or at least incidental, to de-

[16] AUTHOR'S NOTE: The statement is true to such a point that it cannot only be made thus vaguely, but it can be developed by enumerating the precise phases of the progressive fragmentation, in the three generations of the past century and the first generation of the twentieth.

bate as did the philosopher Scheler and the Minister of Education Becker, a few years ago, over the question whether these functions are to be performed by a single institution or by various institutions.[17] It is vain because in the end all these functions would unite in the person of the student: they would all eventually come to gravitate around his adolescent years, as a common center.

The question is different. It is this: Even when instruction is limited, as at present, to professional matter and the methods of science, the result is a fabulous profusion of studies. It is impossible even for the better than ordinary student to come anywhere near real success in learning what the university professes to teach him. But institutions exist—they are necessary and they have meaning—because the ordinary man exists. If there were none but extraordinary creatures, it is very probable that there would be no institutions, either educational or political.[18] It is therefore necessary to consider any institution with reference to the man of ordinary endowment. For him it is made, and he must be its unit of measure.

Let us suppose for a moment that in the university, as it is, we find nothing which deserves to be called an abuse. Everything is running smoothly and properly according to what the university professes itself to be. Very well: even then I should say the university of today is an abuse in itself, because it is, in itself, a falsehood.

It is so thoroughly impossible for the ordinary student to master what the university tries to teach him, that it has become a part of university life to accept the failure. In other

17 EDITOR'S NOTE: See especially Carl Heinrich Becker (by error "Beeker" in the Spanish editions), *Gedanken zur Hochschulreform*, Leipzig: Quelle u. Meyer, 1919; and Max Scheler, "*Innere Widersprüche der deutschen Universitäten*," *Westdeutsche Wochenschrift* 1, 32: 493-495; 33: 511-512; 34: 524-527; 35: 539-541; 36: 551-553.

18 AUTHOR'S NOTE: Anarchy is logical when it declares all institutions to be useless and thus pernicious, for it starts with the postulate that every man is extraordinary by birth—i.e. good, prudent, intelligent, and just.

words, it is taken for granted as a regular thing, that what the university attempts to be is a delusion. We accept the falsity of the university's inward life—its very essence is composed of its own falsification. This is the root of the whole trouble (as it always is in life, individual or collective). The original sin stems from the pretension to be other than one's true self. It is our privilege to *try* to be whatever we wish; but it is vicious to pretend to be what we are not, and to delude ourselves by growing habituated to a radically false idea of what we are. When the habitual behavior of a man or an institution is false, the next step is complete demoralization. And thence to degeneracy, for it is not possible for anyone to submit to the falsification of his nature without losing his self-respect.

That is why Leonardo da Vinci said: "Chi non può quel che vuol, quel che può voglia"—"Who cannot what he will, let him will what he can."

This maxim of Leonardo's must guide from the beginning any real reform of the university. Only a firm resolution to be genuine will bear fruit. And not only the life of the university, but the whole new life must be fashioned by artisans whose first thought is *authenticity*. (Note this, Younger Generation. Otherwise, you are lost. In fact you show signs of being lost already.)

An institution, then, which feigns to give and to require what it cannot, is false and demoralized. Yet this principle of deceit is to be found throughout the whole plan and structure of the present university.

The conclusion seems to me inescapable, that we must turn the present university upside down, so to speak, and stand it upon precisely the opposite principle. Instead of teaching what *ought* to be taught, according to some Utopian desire, we must teach only what *can* be taught; that is, *what can be learned*.

I shall attempt to develop the implications of this formula.

35

The problem extends in reality quite beyond the subject of higher education. It involves the capital question of education at all levels.

What has been the great historic advance in pedagogy? Beyond doubt, the turn it has taken under the inspiration of Rousseau, Pestalozzi, Froebel, and German idealism, amounting to a revolutionary avowal of the obvious. In education there are three elemental factors: what is taught (knowledge, wisdom), and the teacher and the learner. Yet with peculiar blindness, education had centered about knowledge and the teacher. The learner was no factor in pedagogy. The innovation of Rousseau and his successors was simply to shift the center of gravity of the science from knowledge and the teacher to the learner, recognizing that it is the learner and his characteristics which alone can guide us in our effort to make something organic of education. Knowledge and research have their own structure, which is not applicable to that other activity proposing to impart knowledge. The principle of pedagogy is entirely different from that on which culture and science are built.

But we must go a step further. Rather than lose ourselves in a minute study of the learner's characteristics as a child, as a youth, etc., we are constrained to limit the subject for our present purpose, and consider the child and the youth from a more modest point of view, which is more precise: namely, as a student and apprentice. Then we strike upon the fact that it is not the child as a child, or the youth because of his youth, that obliges us to ply this special profession we call "teaching." It is something far less complicated, and in fact, very definite and simple.

Let me explain.

THE PRINCIPLE OF ECONOMY
IN EDUCATION

CHAPTER III

The Principle of Economy in Education

THE science of political economy emerged from the war in much the same shattered state as did the economies of the belligerent nations. There was nothing to do but set about reconstructing this whole body of knowledge from the ground up. Such adventures are as a rule beneficial in the life of a science, for they force it to seek a more solid basis than has been in use, a more general and fundamental principle. And in fact at the present time, political economy is arising from its ruins, for a reason so obvious that it is embarrassing to mention. To wit: that economic *science* necessarily responds to the fundamental principle underlying the economic *activity* of man. Why is it that mankind engages in economic occupations, producing, managing, bartering, saving, appraising, etc.? For one astonishing reason, and that alone: because many of the things man desires and requires are not to be had in unlimited abundance. If all we need existed in plenty and to spare, it would never have occurred to men to fatigue themselves with economic exertion. Air, for example, does not usually give rise to activity we could call economic. Yet as soon as air becomes scarce in some way or other, it immediately occasions economic activity. For example children in a schoolroom need a certain amount of air. If the room is small there is a scarcity of air; hence an economic problem, ending in an enlarged school which is accordingly more expensive.

Again, even though our planet is rolling in air, so to speak, its air is not all of the same quality. "Pure air" is to be had only at certain places, at certain altitudes, under specific conditions of climate. "Pure air" is scarce. And that simple fact provokes an intense economic activity among the Swiss —hotels, sanitariums—converting this scarce raw material into health, at so much per day.

This is all astonishingly simple, I repeat; but it is undeniably true. Scarcity is the basis of economic activity, and indeed the Swedish economist Cassel, some years ago, revised the science of economics by taking as a point of departure the *principle of scarcity*.[1] Einstein has remarked many times that "if perpetual motion existed, there would be no such thing as physics." Similarly, we may be sure that in Elysium there is no economic activity, and consequently no science of economics.

I am persuaded that an analogous situation has its effect in education. Why does pedagogical activity exist at all? Why is it an occupation and a preoccupation of man? To these questions the romantics gave most brilliant, moving, and transcendental answers, in which they drew upon all things human and a good portion of the divine. For their taste, it was always necessary to obscure the bare nature of things with festoons of ornamental foliage, and a touch of melodrama. We, on the contrary—am I not right, young people?—we are content to accept things for what they are (at least for the time being), and nothing more. We like their bareness. We do not mind cold and inclemency. We know that life is hard, and will be hard. We accept the rigor of it; we do not try to sophisticate destiny. Because life is hard, it does not seem to us any the less magnificent. On the contrary, if it is hard it is also solid and sturdy. Above all, it is free of any hypocrisy. We value openness in our dealings with things. We like to strip things bare, and when they are thus denuded, to wash them clean as we examine them, and see what they are *in puris naturalibus.*

[1] AUTHOR'S NOTE: See Gustavo Cassel, *Theoretische Sozialœkonomie*, 1921, pp. 3 ff. In part this amounts to a return to some positions of classic economics, as opposed to the economics of the last sixty years.

Man is occupied and preoccupied with education for a reason which is simple, bald, and devoid of glamour: in order to live with assurance and freedom and efficiency, it is necessary to know an enormous number of things, and the child or youth has an extremely limited capacity for learning. That is the reason. If childhood and youth lasted a century apiece, or if the child and the adolescent possessed intelligence and the power of attention practically without limit, the teaching activity would never exist. Even if those appealing, transcendental reasons had never operated at all, mankind would have had to develop that variety of the species known as the teacher.

Scarcity of the capacity to learn is the cardinal principle of education. It is necessary to provide for teaching precisely in proportion as the learner is unable to learn.

Is it not a too striking coincidence that the ferment in education erupted toward the middle of the eighteenth century, and has continued to increase up to the present? Why did this not happen sooner? The explanation is simple: it was precisely at that time that the first great flowering of modern culture ripened for harvest. In a short time, the treasure of active human knowledge became enlarged by a tremendous increment. Life was entering into the full swing of the new capitalism, which recent inventions had made possible: life was consequently assuming a new and appalling complexity, and it was exacting a greater and greater equipment of technics. Accordingly, along with the necessity for learning a quantity of things quite beyond the capacity to learn, pedagogy was promptly intensified and expanded to meet the need.

In primitive epochs, on the other hand, there is scarcely such a thing as education.[2] Why should there be, if there is

[2] EDITOR's NOTE: The primitive cultures we are able to observe do of course transmit to their youth considerable knowledge of zoology and anatomy, botany, social usage and even philosophy of the differences

scarcely any need for it—if the capacity to learn is far ahead of the material to be assimilated? The capacity is in excess. There are but a few branches of knowledge, certain magic formulas and rituals for fabricating the most difficult instruments, like the canoe, or for curing illness and casting out devils. This is all the subject matter there is. Since it is so scant, anyone could learn it without applying himself with any special effort. Hence there arises a peculiar situation, which corroborates my thesis in the most unexpected fashion. The fact is that education appears among primitive peoples in an inverted form: the vocation of teaching is actually one of concealing. The sacred formulas are conserved as secrets, and passed on esoterically to a chosen few. Outsiders would learn them all too readily. Whence the universal phenomenon of secret rites.

The phenomenon is so persistent that it reappears at any level of civilization, when there arises a particularly novel variety of knowledge, superior in kind to all that has been previously known. Since the new and enviable knowledge exists at first only in small quantity, it is a valuable kind of property, to be imparted only in jealous secrecy. Thus it happened with the Pythagorean school's philosophy of precision, and even with so enlightened a philosopher as Plato. For we have his famous seventh epistle, written with the purpose of protesting against the accusation that he had taught his philosophy to Dionysius of Syracuse, as if that were a heinous crime. All primitive education, in which there is little to teach, is esoteric and secretive; in that respect it is the antithesis of education as we conceive it in our day.

Education comes into being, then, when the knowledge which has to be acquired is out of proportion to the capacity

in tribal cultures. But the point remains valid, that primitive cultures are not confronted with our problem of an unmanageable quantity of important knowledge.

to learn. Today, more than ever before, the profusion of cultural and technical possessions is such that it threatens to bring a catastrophe upon mankind, in as much as every generation is finding it more nearly impossible to assimilate it.

It is urgent therefore that we base our science of teaching, its methods and institutions, upon the plain, humble principle that the child or the youth who is to be the learner cannot learn all we should like him to know—the principle of economy in education.

Since it could not be otherwise, this rule has always been in operation where there has been pedagogical activity; but only because it could not be helped, and hence in a restricted degree. It has never been set up as a principle, perhaps because at first sight it is not dramatic—it does not talk of imposing transcendentals.

The university of today, outside Spain even more than within, is a tropical underbrush of subject matters. If to this we add what we have deemed imperative—the teaching of culture—the verdure threatens to hide the horizon altogether: the horizon of youth which needs to be clear and open, in order that it may expose to view the beckoning glow afar off. There is no remedy but to rise up against this turgid overgrowth and use the principle of economy like a hatchet. First of all, a thorough pruning.

The principle of economy not only implies that it is necessary to economize in the subject matter to be offered. It has a further implication: that the organization of higher education, the construction of the university, must be based upon the student, and not upon the professor or upon knowledge. The university must be the projection of the student to the scale of an institution. And his two dimensions are, first, what he is—a being of limited learning capacity—and second, what he needs to know in order to live his life.

(The present student movement comprises many ingredients. Out of the conventional ten parts, seven are made up of pure buffoonery. But the other three are absolutely reasonable and more than justify the whole student agitation. One is the political unrest of the country: the soul of the nation is perturbed. The second is a series of real though incredible abuses on the part of a few professors. And the third, which is the most important and decisive, influences the students without their realizing it. It is the fact that neither they nor anybody in particular, but the times themselves, the present circumstances in education throughout the world, are forcing the university to center itself once more on the student—to *be* the student, and not the professor, as it was in the heyday of its greatness.[3] The tendencies of the times press on inevitably, though mankind, impelled as it is by them, may be unaware of their presence, and quite unable to define them or give them a name. The students should eliminate the discreditable parts of their activity and emphasize these three, especially the last, for in these they are entirely right.[4])

We must begin, therefore, with the ordinary student, and take as the nucleus of the institution, as its central and basic

[3] EDITOR'S NOTE: This is true of both the Parisian and the Bolognese families of the medieval university. While Paris is said to have had a "magisterial constitution," as opposed to the "student constitution" of the other family, yet even at Paris the students, through their organization in "nations," had a responsible part in the maintenance of discipline and morale.

[4] AUTHOR'S NOTE: The concept that the university *is* the student is to be carried out even to the point of affecting its material organization. It is absurd to consider the university, as it has been considered hitherto, the professor's house in which he receives pupils. Rather the contrary: put the students in charge of the house, and let the student body constitute the torso of the institution, complemented by the faculties of professors. The maintenance of discipline through beadles gives rise to shameful squabbles, and organizes the students into a rebellious horde. The students are not to blame, but the institution, which is badly planned. The students themselves, properly organized for the purpose, should direct the internal ordering of the university, determine the decorum of usages and manners, impose disciplinary measures, and feel responsible for the morale.

portion, *exclusively* the subject matters which can be required with absolute stringency, i.e. those a good ordinary student can really learn.

This, I repeat, is what the university should be, at its very base. Presently we shall see that the university must be, in addition, several other things which are no less important. But what is important at this point is not to confuse things: it is to separate carefully from one another the various functions and organs of that imposing institution, the university.

How are we to determine the body of subjects which are to constitute the torso or *minimum* of the curriculum? By submitting the present conglomeration to two tests:

1. We must pick out that which appears as strictly necessary for the life of the man who is now a student. Life, with its inexorable requirements, is the criterion that should guide this first stroke of the pruning knife.

2. What remains, having been judged strictly necessary, must be further reduced to what the student can really learn with thoroughness and understanding.

It is not enough that this or that is necessary. When we least expect, the necessary suddenly passes beyond the capabilities of the student. It would be fantastic on our part to rant and rave that it is necessary. Only so much must be taught as can truly be learned. On this point we must be unshakable, though the line of action which issues from it is drastic.

WHAT THE UNIVERSITY MUST BE PRIMARILY: THE UNIVERSITY; PROFESSION AND SCIENCE

CHAPTER IV

What the University Must Be Primarily: the University; Profession and Science

By APPLYING the principles we have discussed, we come to the following propositions:

(A) The university consists, primarily and basically, of the higher education which the ordinary man should receive.

(B) It is necessary to make of this ordinary man, first of all, a cultured person: to put him at the height of the times. It follows then, that the primary function of the university is to teach the great cultural disciplines, namely:

1. The physical scheme of the world (Physics).
2. The fundamental themes of organic life (Biology).
3. The historical process of the human species (History).
4. The structure and functioning of social life (Sociology).
5. The plan of the universe (Philosophy).

(C) It is necessary to make the ordinary man a good professional. Besides his apprenticeship to culture, the university will teach him, by the most economical, direct and efficacious procedures intellect can devise, to be a good doctor, a good judge, a good teacher of mathematics or of history. The specific character of this professional teaching must be set aside, however, for fuller discussion.

(D) There is no cogent reason why the ordinary man needs or ought to be a scientist. Scandalous consequence: science in the true sense, i.e. scientific investigation, does not belong in any direct, constituent capacity among the primary

49

functions of the university. It is something independent. In what sense the university is inseparable from science, and must be in addition a place of scientific research, is a question we shall treat further on.

No doubt this heretical opinion will call down on itself the deluge of inanities which always threatens from the horizon, like a cloud with teeming paunch. I realize that there are serious objections against this thesis of mine; but before these are advanced, we shall see erupting that volcano of commonplaces which every man becomes when he speaks on a question he has not thought out beforehand.

The plan of a university which I am expounding requires that you indulgently dispose your mind to distinguish three things, each quite different from the others: namely science, culture, and learned profession. You must renounce that restful light in which all cats are gray.

First let us differentiate between profession and science. Science is not just whatever you will. Obviously, it is not science to buy yourself a microscope or to throw together a laboratory. But *neither is it science to expound, or learn, the content of a science.* In its proper and authentic sense, science is exclusively investigation: the setting up of problems, working at them, and arriving at their solution. From the moment a solution is reached, all that may subsequently be done with the solution is not science.[1] And that is why it is not science to learn or teach a science, or to apply and appropriate science. It may well be best—with what reservations, we shall presently see—for the man entrusted with the teaching of a science to be a scientist at the same time. But that is not absolutely necessary, and as a matter of fact there have been and are prodigious teachers of the sciences who are not

---

[1] AUTHOR'S NOTE: Except to question it afresh, to convert it back to a problem by criticizing it, and hence to repeat the cycle of scientific investigation.

investigators, i.e. scientists. It is sufficient that they *know* their science. But to know is not to investigate. To investigate is to discover a truth, or inversely, to demonstrate an error. To know means to assimilate a truth into one's consciousness, to possess a fact after it has been attained and secured.

At the beginnings of science, in Greece, when there was yet little science to be had ready made, men hardly ran the same risk of confusing it with things which are not science. The words they used to designate science exposed its identity with inquiry, creative work, investigation. Even the contemporaries of Plato and Aristotle lacked any term to match exactly—including its equivocalness—the modern word "science." They spoke of *historia, exétasis, philosophía*, which mean, with one nuance or another, "a learning by inquiry," "a searching out," and "a systematic treatment of a subject, or scientific investigation"—but not "possession of knowledge." The name *philo-sophía* arose, comparatively late, from the effort to distinguish from the usual learning that novel activity which was not to *be learned*, but to *seek* knowledge.[2]

Science is one of the most sublime pursuits and achievements of mankind: more sublime than the university itself, conceived as an educational institution. For science is creation, and teaching aims only to convey what has been created, to digest it and to induce learners to digest it. Science is carried on upon so high a plane that it is necessarily an extremely delicate process. Whether we like it or not, science excludes the ordinary man. It involves a calling most infrequent, and remote from the ordinary run of the human species. The scientist is the monk of modern times.

To pretend that the normal student is a scientist, is at once a ridiculous pretension, which could scarcely have been con-

[2] AUTHOR's NOTE: The term *epistéme* corresponds better to the bundle of meanings included in our words "knowledge" and "understanding." For the astonishment occasioned by the novel term *philosophía*, see Cicero, *Tusculan Disputations*, V, 3.

51

tracted (pretensions are contracted, like colds and other in-
flammations) but for that vice of utopianism, the bane of
the generation just preceding ours. But furthermore it is not
desirable, even under ideal circumstances, that the ordinary
man should be a scientist. If science is one of the highest of
human pursuits, it is not the only one. There are others of
equal dignity, and there is no reason to sacrifice these, dedicating all humanity to science. The sublimity, moreover, belongs to science itself and not to the man of science. His
career is a mode of existence quite as limited and narrow as
another; in fact more so than some you could imagine. Here
I cannot embark on an analysis of what it means to be a
scientist. Nor do I wish to. It would be out of place, and
besides, some of what I should say might appear noisome.
Returning then to the essential matter, let me observe that
up to our time at least, the *real* scientist, considered as a
person, has been with notorious frequency a visionary and
a freak, when he has not been absolutely demented. The real
marvel, the precious thing, is what this very limited person
succeeds in isolating: the pearl, not the oyster that secreted
it. It is futile to idealize the scientist and hold him up as the
model for all men to imitate, without taking into account the
complex circumstances—miraculous, some of them, and some
of them quite unfathomable—which are wont to enter into
the making of the scientist.[3]

The teaching of the professions and the search for truth
must be separated. They must be clearly distinguished one
from the other, both in the minds of the professors and in
the minds of the students. For their present confusion is an
impediment to science. Granted, the apprenticeship to some
professions includes as a very important element the mastery

[3] AUTHOR'S NOTE: It is notorious for example how readily scientists
have always acquiesced in tyrannical governments. This is no cause
for disappointment, nor can it be considered a liability to society. The
cause of it lies in the very nature of the scientist, and is perfectly respectable.

of the systematized content of numerous sciences; but this content is the end result of investigation, and not the investigation itself. As a general principle, the normal student is not an apprentice to science. The physician is learning to effect cures, and as a physician he need not go beyond that. For his purpose, he needs to know the system of physiology current in his day, but he need not be, and in fact cannot be expected to be, a trained physiologist. Why do we persist in expecting the impossible? I cannot understand. I am only disgusted by this itching to delude oneself—"you *have* to have your illusions"—this everlasting delusion of grandeur, this die-hard utopianism of persuading ourselves that we are achieving what we are not. Utopianism results in a pedagogy of self-abuse.

It is the virtue of the child to think in terms of wishes, it is the child's role to make believe. But the virtue of the grown man is to will, and his role is to do and achieve. Now we can achieve things only by concentrating our energy: by limiting ourselves. And in this limiting of ourselves lies the truth and the authenticity of our life. Indeed, all life is destiny: if our existence were unlimited in duration and in the forms it could assume, there would be no "destiny."[4] The authentic life, young people, consists in cheerfully accepting an inexorable destiny—a limitation we cannot alter. It is this state of mind which the mystics, following a profound intuition, used to call "the state of grace." He who has once honestly accepted his destiny, his own limitations, is imperturable. "*Impavidum ferient ruinae.*"

If a man has the calling to be a physician and nothing more, let him not dabble in science. He will but turn science

[4] EDITOR'S NOTE: Ortega's term "destino" presents much the same difficulty as Aristotle's two terms δύναμις and ἐνέργεια, for which English translators have found no satisfying translation. The organism is conceived as being endowed with a specific *potentiality*, whose *realization* constitutes the organism's proper life. The term "destiny," as well as another, will take on the intended meaning as the essay proceeds.

53

into mediocrity. It is enough, in fact it is everything, that he is a good physician. The same holds in my opinion for the man who is to be a good professor of history in a secondary school. Is it not a mistake to confuse him in college by making him think he is going to be an historian? What do you gain? You force him to consume his time in a fragmentary study of techniques necessary to the research of the historian, but irrelevant to the teaching of history. You excuse him from that other task of achieving a clear, organized, comprehensible idea of the general body of human history, which it is his mission to teach.[5]

The trend toward a university dominated by "inquiry" has been disastrous. It has led to the elimination of the prime concern: culture. It has deflected attention from the problem of how best to train future professionals for their professions.

The medical schools aspire to teach physiology and chemistry complete to the nth degree; but perhaps in no medical school the world over is there anyone seriously occupied with thinking out what it really means to be a good physician, what the ideal type should be for our times. The profession, which after culture is the most urgent concern, is entrusted largely to the kindness of Providence. But the harm of our confused procedure has worked both ways. Science too has suffered by our wishful attempt to bring it into line alongside the professions.

Pedantry and the want of reflection have been large causes in bringing on the "scientism" which afflicts the university. In Spain, both these deplorable forces are coming to be a serious nuisance. Any nincompoop that has been six months in a school or a laboratory in Germany or North America, any parrot that has made a third rate scientific discovery, comes back a *nouveau riche* of science. Without having

[5] AUTHOR'S NOTE: It is obvious that he must learn what composes the techniques by which history is obtained. But this does not mean that he must become an adept, himself, in these techniques.

reflected a quarter of an hour on the mission of the university, he propounds the most pedantic and ridiculous reforms. Moreover he is incapable of teaching his own courses, for he has no grasp of the discipline as a whole.

We must therefore shake science off the tree of the professions, and retain only the portion of science which is strictly necessary, in order to attend to the professions themselves, whose teaching, today, runs quite wild. At this step everything is still to be begun.[6]

Logical organization and ingenious teaching will make it possible to teach the professions much more efficiently and with greater breadth, with less time and effort than at present.

But now let us proceed to that other distinction, between science and culture.

[6] AUTHOR'S NOTE: The basic idea, the prototype of each profession— what it means to be a doctor, judge, lawyer, professor, etc.—is not at present delineated in the popular mind, nor does anyone devote himself to studying and formulating such an idea.

55

CULTURE AND SCIENCE

Culture and Science

IF WE review in substance the distinction between profession and science, we find ourselves in possession of a few clear ideas. For example, medicine is not a science but a profession, a matter of practice. Hence it represents a point of view distinct from that of science. It proposes as its object to restore and maintain health in the human species. To this end, it appropriates what it finds useful: it goes to science and takes whatever results of research it considers efficacious; but it leaves all the rest. It leaves particularly what is most characteristic of science: the cultivation of the problematic and doubtful. This would suffice to differentiate radically between medicine and science. Science consists in an urge to solve problems; the more it is engaged in this occupation, the more purely it accomplishes its mission. But medicine exists for the purpose of applying solutions. If they happen to be scientific, so much the better. But they are not necessarily so. They may have grown out of some millennial experience which science has not yet explained or even confirmed.

In the last fifty years, medicine has allowed itself to be swept off its feet by science, it has neglected its own mission and failed to assert properly its own professional point of view.[1] Medicine has committed the besetting sin of that

[1] AUTHOR'S NOTE: On the other hand, when medicine has devoted itself to its proper function of curing, its work has proved most fruitful for science. Contemporary physiology was launched on its career, early in the last century, not by the scientists but by the physicians, who turned aside from the scholasticism that had reigned over eighteenth century biology (taxonomy, anatomism, etc.) to meet their urgent mission with pragmatic theories. See Emanuel Radl, *Geschichte der*

whole period: namely, to look askance at destiny and strain to be something else—in this case, pure science.

Let us make no mistake about it. Science, upon entering into a profession, must be detached from its place in pure science, to be organized upon a new center and a new principle, as professional technics. And if this is true, it must certainly have an effect on the teaching of the professions.

Something similar is to be said of the relations between culture and science. The difference between them seems to me clear enough. Yet I should like not only to leave the concept of culture very definite in the mind of the reader but also to show what basis it has. First, the reader must go to the trouble of scrutinizing and reflecting upon the following résumé—which will not be easy: culture is the system of vital ideas which each age possesses; better yet, it is the system of ideas *by* which the age lives. There is no denying the fact that man invariably lives according to some definite ideas which constitute the very foundation of his way of life. These ideas which I have called "vital," meaning ideas by which an age conducts its life, are no more nor less than the repertory of our *active* convictions as to the nature of our world and our fellow creatures, convictions as to the hierarchy of the values of things—which are more to be esteemed, and which less.[2]

It is not in our hands, whether to possess such a repertory of convictions or not. It is a matter of inescapable necessity, an ingredient essential to every human life, of whatever sort it may be. The reality we are wont to refer to as "human life," your life and the next fellow's, is something quite remote from biology, the science of organisms. Biology, like any other science, is no more than one occupation to which

biologischen Theorien, vol. II (1909), a book which seems the more admirable with the passing of time.

[2] EDITOR'S NOTE: Cf. Ortega's *The Modern Theme,* p. 76: "Culture is merely a special direction which we give to the cultivation of our animal potencies."

some men devote their "life." The basic and truest meaning of the word *life* is not biological but biographical: and that is the meaning it has always had in the language of the people. It means the totality of what we do and what we are—that formidable business, which every man must exercise on his own, of maintaining a place in the scheme of things and steering a course among the beings of the world. "To live is, in fact, to have dealing with the world: to address oneself to it, exert oneself in it, and occupy oneself with it."[3] If these actions and occupations which compose our living were produced in us mechanically, the result would not be human life. The automaton does not *live*. The whole difficulty of the matter is that life is not given us ready made. Like it or not, we must go along from instant to instant, deciding for ourselves. At each moment it is necessary to make up our minds what we are going to do next: the life of man is an ever recurrent problem. In order to decide at one instant what he is going to do or to be at the next, man is compelled to form a plan of some sort, however simple or puerile it may be. It is not that he *ought* to make a plan. There is simply no possible life, sublime or mean, wise or stupid, which is not essentially characterized by its proceeding with reference to some plan.[4] Even to abandon our life to chance, in a moment of despair, is to make a plan. Every human being, perforce, picks his way through life. Or what comes to the same, as he decides upon each act he performs, he does so *because* that act "seems best," given the circumstances. This is tantamount to saying that every life is obliged, willy-nilly, to justify itself in its own eyes. Self-justification is a constituent part of our

[3] AUTHOR'S NOTE: I have borrowed this formula from my essay *El Estado, la juventud y el carnaval*, published in *La Nación*, of Buenos Aires, December 1924, and reprinted in *El Espectador* (VII).

[4] AUTHOR'S NOTE: The sublimity or meanness of a life, its wisdom or stupidity is, precisely, its plan. Obviously our plan does not remain the same for life; it may vary continually. The essential fact is that life and plan are inseparable.

life. We refer to one and the same fact, whether we say that "to live is to conduct oneself according to a plan," or that "life is a continuous justification to oneself." But this plan or justification implies that we have acquired some "idea" of the world and the things in it, and also of our potential acts which have bearing upon it. In short, man cannot live without reacting to his environment with some rudimentary concept of it. He is forced to make an intellectual interpretation of the world about him, and of his conduct in it. This interpretation is the repertory of ideas or convictions to which I have referred, and which, as it is now perfectly evident, cannot be lacking in any human life whatsoever.[5]

The vast majority of these convictions or ideas are not fabricated by the individual, Crusoe-wise, but simply received by him from his historical environment—his times. Naturally, any age presents very disparate systems of convictions. Some are a drossy residue of other times. But there is always a system of live ideas which represents the superior level of the age, a system which is essentially characteristic of its times; and this system is the culture of the age. He who lives at a lower level, on archaic ideas, condemns himself to a lower life, more difficult, toilsome, unrefined. This is the plight of backward peoples—or individuals. They ride through life in an ox-cart while others speed by them in automobiles. Their concept of the world wants truth, it wants richness, and it wants acumen. The man who lives on a plane beneath the enlightened level of his time is condemned, relatively, to the life of an infra-man.

[5] AUTHOR'S NOTE: It is easy to see that when an element of our life so fundamental as this self-justification functions irregularly, the ailment which ensues is grave. Such is the case with the curious type of man I have studied in *The Revolt of the Masses*. But the first edition of that book is incomplete. A prolonged illness prevented me from finishing it. In the later editions [not yet appeared, Oct. 1944—Ed.] I am adding the third part of the study, analyzing more in detail this formidable problem of "justification," and thus adding the finishing touch to that book's investigation into this very prevalent phenomenon.

In our age, the content of culture comes largely from science. But our discussion suffices to indicate that culture is not science. The content of culture, though it is being made in the field of science more than elsewhere, is not scientific fact but rather a vital faith, a conviction characteristic of our times. Five hundred years ago, faith was reposed in ecclesiastical councils, and the content of culture emanated in large part from them.

Culture does with science, therefore, the same thing the profession does. It borrows from science what is vitally necessary for the interpretation of our existence. There are entire portions of science which are not culture, but pure scientific technique. And vice versa, culture requires that we possess a complete concept of the world and of man; it is not for culture to stop, with science, at the point where the methods of absolute theoretic rigor happen to end. Life cannot wait until the sciences may have explained the universe scientifically. We cannot put off living until we are ready. The most salient characteristic of life is its coerciveness: it is always urgent, "here and now" without any possible postponement. Life is fired at us point-blank. And culture, which is but its interpretation, cannot wait any more than can life itself.

This sharpens the distinction between culture and the sciences. Science is not something by which we live. If the physicist had to live by the ideas of his science, you may rest assured that he would not be so finicky as to wait for some other investigator to complete his research a century or so later. He would renounce the hope of a complete scientific solution, and fill in, with approximate or probable anticipations, what the rigorous corpus of physical doctrine lacks at present, and in part, always will lack.

The internal conduct of science is not a *vital* concern; that of culture is. Science is indifferent to the exigencies of our life, and follows its own necessities. Accordingly, science grows constantly more diversified and specialized without

63

limit, and is never completed. But culture is subservient to our life here and now, and is required to be, at every instant, a complete, unified, coherent system—the plan of life, the path leading through the forest of existence.

That metaphor of ideas as paths or roads (*méthodoi*) is as old as culture itself. Its origin is evident. When we find ourselves in a perplexing, confused situation, it is as though we stood before a dense forest, through whose tangles we cannot advance without being lost. Someone explains the situation, with a happy idea, and we experience a sudden illumination —the "light" of understanding. The thicket immediately appears ordered, and the lines of its structure seem like paths opening through it. Hence the term *method* is regularly associated with that of enlightenment, illumination, *Aufklärung*. What we call today "a cultured man" was called more than a century ago "an enlightened man," i.e. a man who sees the paths of life in a clear light.

Let us cast away once for all those vague notions of enlightenment and culture, which make them appear as some sort of ornamental accessory for the life of leisure. There could not be a falser misrepresentation. Culture is an indispensable element of life, a dimension of our existence, as much a part of man as his hands. True, there is such a thing as man without hands; but that is no longer simply man: it is man crippled. The same is to be said of life without culture, only in a much more fundamental sense. It is a life crippled, wrecked, false. The man who fails to live at the height of his times is living beneath what would constitute his right life. Or in other words, he is swindling himself out of his own life.

We are passing at present, despite certain appearances and presumptions, through an age of terrific *un-culture*. Never perhaps has the ordinary man been so far below his times and what they demand of him. Never has the civilized world so abounded in falsified, cheated lives. Almost nobody is poised squarely upon his proper and authentic place in life.

Man is habituated to living on subterfuges with which he deceives himself, conjuring up around him a very simple and arbitrary world, in spite of the admonitions of an active conscience which forces him to observe that his real world, the world that corresponds to the whole of actuality, is one of enormous complexity and grim urgency. But he is afraid—our ordinary man is timorous at heart, with all his brave gesticulations—he is afraid to admit this real world, which would make great demands on him. He prefers to falsify his life, and keep it sealed up in the cocoon of his fictitious, oversimplified concept of the world.[6]

Hence the historic importance of restoring to the university its cardinal function of "enlightenment," the task of imparting the full culture of the time and revealing to mankind, with clarity and truthfulness, that gigantic world of today in which the life of the individual must be articulated, if it is to be authentic.

Personally, I should make a Faculty of Culture the nucleus of the university and of the whole higher learning.[7] I have

[6] AUTHOR'S NOTE: On this subject in general see *The Revolt of the Masses* in its next edition [not yet published, Oct. 1944—ED.], where I deal more in detail with the specific ways in which the people of today are falsifying their lives: for example, the naive belief that "you have to be arbitrary," from which has issued in politics the lie of Fascism, and in letters and philosophy, the young Spanish "intellectual" of recent years.

[7] EDITOR'S NOTE: The form of this proposal has been objected to by readers of the manuscript, on the ground that it gives too much responsibility and too much power to one group. The American college or university might better seek to solve the administrative problem through a committee representative of the whole faculty, serving as the spearhead for the reform yet democratically stimulating and coordinating the initiative arising from all parts of the institution. Another committee of the whole faculty might be made responsible to improve the conditions for research; and each professional department might appoint a committee of appropriate academic and community representatives to examine how the occupational training can be oriented toward a richer service to society. This adaptation of Ortega's basic idea has been elaborated in the editor's forthcoming book on cultural education and intercultural synthesis, tentatively scheduled to be published in 1945 by Harper and Brothers.

already sketched the outline of its disciplines. Each of these, it will be remembered, bears two names: for example "The physical scheme of the world (Physics)." This dual designation is intended to suggest the difference between a cultural discipline, vitally related to life, and the corresponding science by which it is nurtured. The "Faculty" of Culture would not expound physics as the science is presented to a student intending to devote his life to physico-mathematical research. The physics in culture is the rigorously derived synthesis of ideas about the nature and functioning of the physical cosmos, as these ideas have emerged from the physical research so far completed. In addition, this discipline will analyze the means of acquiring knowledge, by which the physicist has achieved his marvelous construction; it will therefore be necessary to expound the principles of physics, and to trace, briefly but scrupulously, the course of their historical evolution. This last element of the course will enable the student to visualize what the "world" was, in which man lived a generation or a century or a thousand years ago; and by contrast, he will be able to realize and appreciate the peculiarities of our "world" of today.

This is the time to answer an objection which arose at the beginning of my essay, and was postponed. How—it is asked —can the present day concept of matter be made intelligible to anyone who is not versed in higher mathematics? Every day, mathematical method makes some new advance at the very base of physical science.

I should like the reader to consider the tragedy without escape which would confront humanity if the view implied here were correct. Either everyone would be obliged to be a thorough physicist, devoting himself, dedicating his life,[8] to research in order not to live inept and devoid of insight into the world we live in; or else most of us must resign our-

---

[8] AUTHOR'S NOTE: It is to be noted that any dedicating of oneself, if it is real, means the dedication of one's life and nothing less.

selves to an existence which, in one of its dimensions, is doomed to stupidity. The physicist would be for the man in the street like some being endowed with a magical, hieratical knowledge. Both of these solutions would be—among other things—ridiculous.

But fortunately there is no such dilemma. In the first place, the doctrine I am defending calls for a thorough rationalizing of the methods of instruction, from the primary grades to the university. Precisely by recognizing science to be a thing apart, we pave the way to the segregating of its cultural elements so that these may be made assimilable. The "principle of economy in education" is not satisfied by extruding disciplines the student cannot learn; it requires economy in the teaching of what remains to be taught. Economy in these two respects would add a new margin to the learning capacity of the student, so that he could actually learn more than at present.[9] I believe, then, that in time to come no student will arrive at the university without being already acquainted with the mathematics of physics, sufficiently at least to be capable of understanding its formulas.

Mathematicians exaggerate a bit the difficulties of their subject. It is an extensive one but, after all, it is always expressible in definite terms to anyone who "knows beans." If it appears so incomprehensible today, it is because the necessary energy has not been applied to the simplifying of its teaching. This affords me an opportunity to proclaim for the first time, and with due solemnity, that if we fail to cultivate this sort of intellectual effort—effort addressed not to descriptive analysis, after the usual manner of research, but to the task of simplifying, and synthesizing the quintessence of science, without sacrifice of its quality or substantialness—then the future of science itself will be disastrous.

It is imperative that the present dispersion and complica-

[9] AUTHOR'S NOTE: Precisely because of the efficiency in the teaching, a greater power to learn is called into action.

tion of scientific labors be counterbalanced by the complementary kind of scientific activity, striving toward the concentration and consolidation of knowledge. We need to develop a special type of talent, for the specific function of synthesizing. The destiny of science is at stake.

But, in the second place, I deny roundly that in order to grasp the fundamental ideas—the principles, the methods of procedure, the end results—of any science which has fundamental ideas to offer, the student must necessarily have had formal training and become familiar with its techniques. The truth is quite otherwise. When a science, in its internal development, proceeds toward ideas which require technical familiarity in order to be understood, then its ideas are losing their fundamental character to become instruments subordinate to the science, rather than its substance proper.[10] The mastery of higher mathematics is essential for *making* the science but not for understanding its import for human life.

It happens, at once luckily and unluckily, that the nation which stands gloriously and indisputably in the van of science is Germany. The German, in addition to his prodigious talent and inclination for science, has a congenital weakness which it would be extremely hard to extirpate: he is *a nativitate* pedantic and impervious of mind. This fact has brought it about that not a few sides of our present-day science are not really science, but only pedantic detail, all too easily and credulously gathered together. One of the tasks Europe needs to perform with dispatch is to rid contemporary science of its purely German excrescences, its rituals and mere whims, in order to save its essential parts uncontaminated.[11]

[10] AUTHOR'S NOTE: In the last analysis, mathematics is wholly instrumental in character, not fundamental or substantial in itself—just as is that branch of science which studies the microscope.

[11] AUTHOR'S NOTE: Do not forget, in seeking to grasp the implications of this opinion, that the writer of it owes to Germany four fifths of his intellectual possessions. I am more conscious today than ever

68

Europe cannot be saved without a return to intellectual discipline, and this discipline needs to be more rigorous than those which have been used or abused in other times. No one must be allowed to escape. Not even the man of science. Today this personage conserves not a little of feudal violence, egotism and arrogance, vanity and pontification.

There is need to humanize the scientist, who rebelled, about the middle of the last century, and to his shame let himself be contaminated by the gospel of insubordination which has been thenceforth the great vulgarity and the great falsity of the age.[12] The man of science can no longer afford to be what he now is with lamentable frequency—a barbarian knowing much of one thing. Fortunately the principal figures in the present generation of scientists have felt impelled by the internal necessities of their sciences to balance their specialization with a symmetrical culture. The rest will follow in their steps as sheep follow the leading ram.

From all quarters the need presses upon us for a new integration of knowledge, which today lies in pieces scattered over the world. But the labor of this undertaking is enormous; it is not to be thought of while there exists no methodology of higher education even comparable to what we have for the preceding levels of education. At present we lack completely a pedagogy of the university—though this statement seems untrue at first.

It has come to be an imminent problem, one which mankind can no longer evade, to invent a technique adequate to cope with the accumulation of knowledge now in our posses-

before of the indisputable, towering preeminence of German science. The question alluded to has nothing to do with this.

12 AUTHOR'S NOTE: The great task of the present age, in the field of morality, is to convince common men (uncommon men never fell into the snare) of the inane foolishness which envelops this urge to revolt, and make them see the cheap facility, the meanness of it; even though we may freely admit that most of the things revolted against deserve to be buried away. The only true revolt is creation—the revolt against nothingness. Lucifer is the patron saint of mere negativistic revolt.

sion. Unless some practicable way is found to master this exuberant growth, man will eventually become its victim. On top of the primitive forest of life we would only add the forest of science, whose intention was to simplify the first. If science has brought order into life we shall now have to put science in order, organize it—seeing that it is impossible to regiment science—for the sake of its healthy perpetuation. To this end we must vitalize science: that is, we must provide it with a form compatible with the human life by which and for which it was made in the first place. Otherwise—for there is no use to entrench ourselves behind a vague optimism—otherwise science will cease to function; mankind will lose interest in it.

And so you see that by thinking over what is the mission of the university, by seeking to discover the consequent character of its cultural disciplines (viz. systematic and synthetic), we come out upon a vast horizon that spreads quite beyond the field of pedagogy, and engages us to see in the institution of higher learning an agent for the salvation of science itself.

The need to create sound syntheses and systematizations of knowledge, to be taught in the "Faculty of Culture," will call out a kind of scientific genius which hitherto has existed only as an aberration: the genius for integration. Of necessity this means specialization, as all creative effort inevitably does; but this time, the man will be specializing in the construction of a whole. The momentum which impels investigation to dissociate indefinitely into particular problems, the pulverization of research, makes necessary a compensative control—as in any healthy organism—which is to be furnished by a force pulling in the opposite direction, constraining centrifugal science in a wholesome organization.

Men endowed with this genius come nearer being good professors than those who are submerged in their research.

One of the evils attending the confusion of the university with science has been the awarding of professorships, in keeping with the mania of the times, to research workers who are nearly always very poor professors, and regard their teaching as time stolen away from their work in the laboratory or the archives. This was brought home to me by experience, during my years of study in Germany. I have lived close to a good number of the foremost scientists of our time, yet I have not found among them a single good teacher[13]—just so that no one will come and tell me that the German university, as an institution, is a model!

[13] AUTHOR's NOTE: Which does not mean that none exist; but it does indicate that the combination does not occur with any dependable frequency.

WHAT THE UNIVERSITY MUST BE "IN ADDITION"

CHAPTER VI

What the University Must Be "In Addition"

THE "principle of economy," which amounts to the determination to see things as they are and not as a Utopian illusion, has led us to define the primary mission of the university in this wise:

1. University, in the strict sense, is to mean that institution which teaches the ordinary student to be a cultured person and a good member of a profession.

2. The university will not tolerate in its program any false pretense: it will profess to require of the student only what actually can be required of him.

3. It will consequently avoid causing the ordinary student to waste part of his time in pretending that he is going to be a scientist. To this end, scientific investigation proper is to be eliminated from the core or minimum of the university.

4. The cultural disciplines and the professional studies will be offered in a rationalized form based on the best pedagogy —systematic, synthetic, and complete—and not in the form which science would prefer, if it were left to itself: special problems, "samples" of science, and experimentation.

5. The selection of professors will depend not on their rank as investigators but on their talent for synthesis and their gift for teaching.

6. When the student's apprenticeship has been reduced to the minimum, both quantitatively and qualitatively, the university will be inflexible in its requirement of him.

This ascetic frugality of pretensions, this severe loyalty in recognizing the limits of the attainable, will, in my belief, procure what is the university's most fundamental need: the need that its institutional life correspond squarely to its proper functions and true limits, in order that its life may be genuine and sincere in its inmost dealings. I have already proposed that the new life should take as its point of departure this simple recognition of the destiny of the individual or of the institution. All else that we may subsequently wish to make of ourselves, or of private institutions or the state, will take root and come to fruition only if we have planted its seed in the rich soil of a nature resigned to be, first of all, the essential minimum which corresponds to its destiny. Europe is sick because its people profess to stand upon a precarious tenth rung in life, without having taken the trouble first to secure a footing on the elemental one, two, three. Destiny is the only bedrock on which human life and all its aspirations can stand. Life on any other basis is false. It has no authentic personality, it is something up in the air. It lacks a local habitation and a name.

Now we can open our minds without fear or reservation, to consider all that the university should be "in addition."

Indeed, the university, such as we have defined it for the nonce, cannot be that alone. And now is the proper time for us to recognize, in all its breadth and depth, the role science must play in the physiology of the university, or rather let us say its psychology, for the university is better to be compared with a spirit than a body.

In the first place, we have seen that culture and profession are not science, but are largely nourished by science. Without science, the destiny of the European man would be an impossibility. The European man represents, in the panorama of history, the being resolved to live according to his intellect; and science is but intellect "in form." Is it perchance a mere accident that only Europe has possessed universities, among so many peoples? The university *is* the intellect, it *is* science, erected into an institution. And this institutionalizing of intellect is the originality of Europe compared with

76

other races, other lands, and other ages. It signifies the peculiar resolution adopted by the European man, to live according to the dictates of his intelligence. Others have chosen to live according to other faculties. Remember the marvelous laconisms in which Hegel sums up universal history, like an alchemist reducing tons of carbon to a few diamonds: Persia, land of Light! (referring to mystical religion); Greece, land of Grace! India, land of Dream! Rome, land of Empire![1]

Europe is the intelligence. A wonderful power: it is the only power which perceives its own limitations—and thereby it proves how intelligent it is! This power which is its own restraint finds in science the scope for its full grandeur.

If culture and the professions were to be isolated in the university and have no contact with the incessant ferment of science, of investigation of all sorts, it would not be long before they would be overtaken by the creeping paralysis of scholasticism. Around the central part of the university, the sciences must pitch their camps—their laboratories and seminars and discussion centers. The sciences are the soil out of which the higher learning grows and from which it draws its sustenance. Accordingly its roots must reach out to the laboratories of every sort and tap them for the nourishment they can provide. All normal university students will come and go between the university and these outlying camps of the sciences, where they will find courses conceived from an exclusively scientific point of view, on all things human and divine. Of the professors, those who are more amply gifted will be investigators as well, and the others, who are purely teachers, will work none the less in closest contact with science, under its criticism and the influence of its ferment and stimulation. What is inadmissible is the confusion of the central portion of the university with the zone of research sur-

[1] AUTHOR'S NOTE: Hegel, *Lectures on the Philosophy of History* (translated from the third German edition by J. Sibree, London, 1861: see pp. xxix ff.).

77

rounding its borders. The university and the laboratory are distinct, correlative organs in a complete physiology. The essential difference between them is that only the university proper is to be characterized as an institution. Science is an activity too sublime and subtle to be organized in an institution. Science is neither to be coerced nor regimented. Hence it is harmful, both for the higher learning and for investigation, to attempt to fuse them into one instead of letting them work hand in hand in an exchange of influence as free and spontaneous as it is intense.

Thus the university is distinct from science yet inseparable from it. I should say myself, "The university *is* science *in addition.*"

Not, however, the simple "addition" of an increment set down in merely external proximity to the institution. Quite the contrary.—And now we may make the point without fear of misunderstanding. The university must *be* science before it can be a university. An atmosphere charged with enthusiasm, the exertion of science, is the presupposition at the base of the university's existence. Precisely because the institution cannot be composed of science—the unrestricted creation of exact knowledge—it requires the spirit of science to animate its institutional life. Unless this spirit is presupposed, all that has been said in the present essay has no sense. Science is the dignity of the university—and more, for life is possible without dignity: it is the soul of the institution, the principle which gives it the breath of life and saves it from being an automaton. That is the sense in which the university "is science, in addition."

But it is still more.[2] Not only does it need perpetual contact with science, on pain of atrophy, it needs contact, likewise, with the public life, with historical reality, with the

[2] AUTHOR'S NOTE: I have deliberately refrained in this essay from even naming the topic of moral education in the university, in order to devote undivided attention to the problem of intellectual content.

present, which is essentially a whole to be dealt with only in its totality, not after amputations *ad usum Delphini.* The university must be open to the whole reality of its time. It must be in the midst of real life, and saturated with it.

And all this not only because it suits the purpose of the university to live in the quickening atmosphere of historical reality. Conversely as well, the life of the people needs acutely to have the university participate, *as* the university, in its affairs.

On this point there is much I should like to say. But to be brief, let me simply allude to the fact that in the collective life of society today there is no other "spiritual power" than the press. The corporate life, which is the real life of history,[3] needs always to be directed, whether we like the idea or not. Of itself it has no form, no eyes to see with, no guiding sense of direction. Now then, in our times, the ancient "spiritual powers" have disappeared: the Church because it has abandoned the present (whereas the life of the people is ever a decidedly current affair); and the state because with the triumph of democracy, it has given up governing the life of the people to be governed instead by their opinion. In this situation, the public life has devolved into the hands of the only spiritual force which necessarily concerns itself with current affairs—the press.

I should not wish to throw too many stones at the journalists; among other motives, there is the consideration that I may be nothing more than a journalist myself. But it is futile

[3] EDITOR'S NOTE: Sr. Ortega has discussed this concept—that "cultures are organisms and are the true subjects for history"—in *Las Atlántidas* (Madrid, 1924), especially p. xxiv, and in the foreword which he wrote for the Spanish edition of Spengler's *Decline of the West.* Sr. Ortega mentions that he had arrived at the concept independently of Spengler. For a discussion of the difficulties that have since discredited the conception of a society as an organism, see Melvin Rader, *No Compromise* (Macmillan, 1939), pp. 239 ff. and 306 ff. See also the essays of Ortega assembled by Mrs. Helene Weyl in *Toward a Philosophy of History,* New York: W. W. Norton, 1941.

to shut our eyes to the obvious fact that spiritual realities differ in worth. They compose a hierarchy of values, and in this hierarchy, journalism occupies an inferior place. It has come to pass that today no pressure and no authority make themselves felt in the public consciousness, save on the very low spiritual plane adopted by the emanations of the press. So low a plane it is that not infrequently the press falls quite short of being a spiritual power, and is rather the opposite force. By the default of other powers, the responsibility for nourishing and guiding the public soul has fallen to the journalist, who not only is one of the least cultured types in contemporary society but who moreover—for reasons I hope may prove to have been merely transitory—admits into his profession the frustrated pseudo-intellectuals, full of resentment and hatred toward what is truly spiritual. Furthermore the journalist's profession leads him to understand by the reality of the times that which creates a passing sensation, regardless of what it is, without any heed for perspective or architecture. Real life is, certainly, purely of the present; but the journalist deforms this truism when he reduces the present to the momentary, and the momentary to the sensational. The result is that, in the public consciousness today, the image of the world appears exactly upside down. The space devoted to people and affairs in the press is inversely proportionate to their substantial and enduring importance; what stands out in the columns of the newspapers and magazines is what will be a "success" and bring notoriety. Were the periodicals to be freed from motives that are often unspeakable; were the dailies kept chastely aloof from any influence of money in their opinions—the press would still, of itself, forsake its proper mission and paint the world inside out. Not a little of the grotesque and general upset of our age— (for Europe has been going along for some time now with her head on the ground and her plebeian feet waving in the air)—is the result of this unchallenged sway of the press as sole "spiritual power."

It is a question of life and death for Europe to put this ridiculous situation to rights. And if this is to be done the university must intervene, *as* the university, in current affairs, treating the great themes of the day from its own point of view: cultural, professional, and scientific.[4] Thus it will not be an institution exclusively for students, a retreat *ad usum Delphini*. In the thick of life's urgencies and its passions, the university must assert itself as a major "spiritual power," higher than the press, standing for serenity in the midst of frenzy, for seriousness and the grasp of intellect in the face of frivolity and unashamed stupidity.

Then the university, once again, will come to be what it was in its grand hour: an uplifting principle in the history of the western world.

[4] AUTHOR'S NOTE: It is inconceivable, for example, that in the face of a problem such as that of foreign exchange, which now preoccupies Spain, the university should not be offering the serious public a course on this difficult economic question.